WEST MIDLANDS
FOOTBALL

WEST MIDLANDS
FOOTBALL

TONY MATTHEWS

TEMPUS

First published 2004

Tempus Publishing Limited
The Mill, Brimscombe Port,
Stroud, Gloucestershire, GL5 2QG
www.tempus-publishing.com

British Library Cataloguing in Publication Data.
A catalogue record for this book is available from the British Library.

ISBN 0 7524 3270 2

Typesetting and origination by Tempus Publishing Limited.
Printed and bound in Great Britain.

Contents

Acknowledgements

 I have been lucky, over the years, to have acquired from various sources, hundreds of photographs, programmes and books, plus other bits of memorabilia appertaining to the wonderful game of football. As a result I have been able to feature an interesting selection of items in this book. A lot are from my personal collection while several more have come from other Midland soccer enthusiasts who have either loaned, sold, donated, presented and/or exchanged the odd item from their own collections as well as adding a few words and facts to my picture captions.

   Therefore, I say thank you to the following: Albion fan Robert Aiken, Roger Baker and Ivan Barnsley (representing Birmingham City), photographer Lee Biddle (Albion), Dave Drage (Birmingham City), statistician John Farrelly and David Goodyear (both Aston Villa), photographer Kevin Grice (Albion), the Wolves duo of Graham Hughes (historian) and programme collector John Hendley, three of my long-time Baggie-buddies, Colin Mackenzie and London-based photographers Barry Marsh and Laurie Rampling, Terry Price (Albion), Graham Silk (Albion), Reg Thacker (former curator of the Villa Park museum), Albion supporter Dean Walton and finally Paul Yeomans (Aston Villa).

   I would also like to say thank you to James Howarth of Tempus Publishing for agreeing to publish my latest book and to my darling wife, Margaret, who still lets me sit down in front of the computer, tip-tapping away on the keyboard hour after hour. It will end some time dear...

Introduction

Football was first played in the West Midlands region more than 130 years ago and the first big-named club to be formed was Aston Villa (1874), followed by near neighbours Birmingham City – initially as Small Heath (in 1875) – then Wolverhampton Wanderers (1877), West Bromwich Albion (1878) and, finally, Walsall (1888).

Villa were one of the best teams around during the early days and were in fact the first Midlands club to win the FA Cup, beating Albion in the 1887 final. But they were pushed hard after that by Albion, who gained revenge with a victory in the 1892 FA Cup final only for Villa to lift the trophy again, once more at Albion's expense, in 1895. Wolves first won the trophy in 1893, while Blues and Walsall have yet to taste the ultimate success in this great competition.

Villa, Wolves and Albion were all founder members of the Football League in 1888. Blues and Walsall quickly joined the action and although the Saddlers slipped out of the competition for a while before the First World War, they have been loyal members ever since (although they are yet to play in the top flight). Villa have been Champions on seven occasions, their last success coming in 1981; Wolves lifted the star prize three times in the 1950s, while Albion were winners in 1920.

Villa, Birmingham, Albion and Wolves have all enjoyed success in the League Cup and Villa have gone further when they became Champions of Europe in 1982. Walsall have not been without honours, although these have mainly come about while gaining promotion.

All five Midland clubs have been blessed with some brilliant footballers. There are far too many to list here, but most of them are featured in this unique book, along with details of many of the top achievements and bitter disappointments. Enjoy what is before you – and recall some of the good old days when footballers played for the love of the game.

Tony Matthews
October 2004

one

In the Beginning

WEST BROMWICH
Albion Football Club.

SEASON TICKET.

1883-1884.

To Admit to all Matches on the

FOUR ACRES,

SITUATE IN SEAGAR STREET.

THREE SHILLINGS.

FOLLOW THE SADDLERS WITH SANDY

BIRMING

FOOTBALL.

THE FIRST

GENERAL MEETING

OF THE

GOLDTHORN

FOOTBALL CLUB

Will (by the kind permission of the Vicar) be held at

ST. LUKE'S SCHOOL

BLAKENHALL,

ON

Friday next, November 10

AT 7 30 PM.

Any Gentleman interested in the game is invited to attend.

PLAYER'S CIGARE

SPENCER

REYNOLDS
WHITEHOUSE
EVANS

ATHERSMITH
COWAN ?????
CRABTREE

DEVEY
CAMPBELL
COWAN ????

WILCOX

ASSOCIATION CUP WINNERS
ASTON VILLA 1897

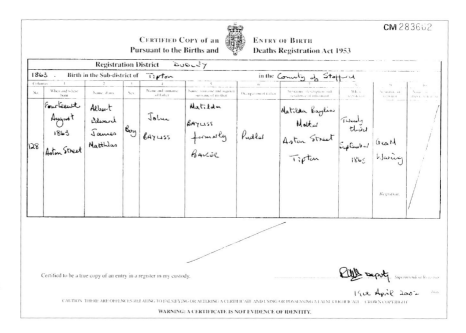

A copy of Jem Bayliss's birth certificate.

Below: One of the first real action pictures taken during an FA Cup final featured 'Gentleman' Jem Bayliss, born in Tipton, who is seen here heading for goal against Aston Villa in the 1887 showdown at The Oval. Villa won the game 2-0, but Albion (who were beaten in the 1886 final by Blackburn Rovers after a replay) later gained sweet revenge over their near neighbours. Bayliss, who also played for England, later became an Albion director. He scored 36 goals in 95 first-class matches for Albion, whom he served as a player from 1884 to 1892.

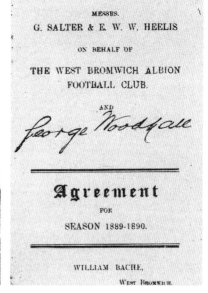

Above right: This is the contract of George Woodhall, who also played for England (*v.* Wales and Scotland in 1888). He helped Albion – fielding an all-English XI who were all born in the Midlands – win the FA Cup that year, scoring in their 2-1 final win over Preston North End at The Oval. He joined Wolves after notching 20 goals in 74 competitive games during his nine years with Albion (1883-92).

Albion's Billy Bassett (left) was born and bred in West Bromwich, and Derby County's Steve Bloomer (a native of Cradley Heath) played together for England on four occasions during the 1890s. Bassett served Albion for fifty-one years as a player (1886–99), coach (after retiring), director (1905–08) and chairman (1908–37). He scored 77 goals in 311 matches, gained two FA Cup winner's medals (1888 and 1892), a runners–up prize in the same competition (1895), and was rewarded with 16 international caps. He was sixty-eight when he died shortly before Albion's FA Cup semi-final with Preston in 1937 (lost 4–1). Bloomer, surprisingly missed by all the Black Country clubs (and others around the Midlands), scored 28 goals in 23 internationals for England and was one of the greatest marksmen of his era.

Having lost to Aston Villa in the 1887 FA Cup final, five years later Albion gained sweet revenge over their near neighbours when they defeated them 3-0 in the 1892 final at The Crystal Palace (which attracted a then record crowd of 32,710). This is the programme produced for that event, showing the heads of all the participating players. Outside left Jasper Geddes, centre forward Sam Nicholls and right half John Reynolds, who later played for Villa, scored the goals.

This was the telegram sent from The Oval, London back to West Bromwich confirming Albion's FA Cup final triumph over Aston Villa in 1892.

John 'Baldy' Reynolds had the honour of playing international football for two different countries. He won 5 caps for Ireland before it was discovered he had been born in Blackburn, thus allowing him to go on and represent England 8 times after that. He was an FA Cup winner with Albion in 1892 (scoring against Villa in the final) and with Aston Villa in 1895 (ironically against Albion). He was also a key member of Villa's double-winning side of 1896/97, having gained his first League Championship medal in 1894. Reynolds, who was as tough as they come, had the pleasure of scoring Albion's first penalty in League football against Nottingham Forest in April 1893.

One of Aston Villa's greatest ever players, Archie Hunter scored 42 goals in 73 senior appearances for the club whom he served for twelve years from 1878. A brilliant individualist, with a commanding personality, he skippered the side to victory in the 1887 FA Cup final (*v*. Albion). A sportsman to the last, he was born almost next door to the poet Robert Burns at Joppa, Ayrshire. Hunter suffered a heart attack playing against Everton in January 1890. Tragically, he never recovered and died four years later, aged thirty-five.

An 1890s advertisement submitted by W.M. Shillcock of 73 Newtown Row, Birmingham, showing items for sale appertaining to football. After Aston Villa had won the FA Cup in 1895 the trophy was placed on display in the front window of Shillcock's shop. Soon afterwards, to the amazement of the club, the shop proprietor and the local police, the trophy was stolen and never recovered.

PLAYER'S CIGARETTES

BAUGH

SWIFT

ROSE

MALPASS

KINSEY

ALLEN

TOPHAM (R.)

GRIFFIN

BUTCHER

WYKES

WOOD

ASSOCIATION CUP WINNERS
WOLVERHAMPTON WANDERERS, 1893

In 1893 Wolverhampton Wanderers (formed in 1877) became the third Midland club to win the FA Cup when they defeated Everton 1-0 at Fallowfield (Manchester), Harry Allen scoring the all-important goal. En route to the final Wolves knocked out Bolton Wanderers, Middlesbrough, Darwen and Blackburn Rovers. They fielded an unchanged side throughout the competition. This is a John Player & Sons cigarette card showing the eleven players who did Wolves proud.

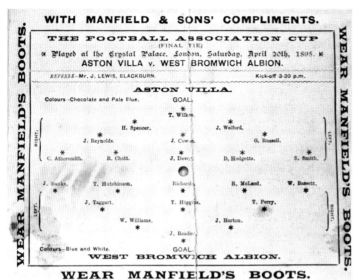

THE FOOTBALL ASSOCIATION CUP
(FINAL TIE)
Played at the Crystal Palace, London, Saturday, April 20th, 1895.
ASTON VILLA v. WEST BROMWICH ALBION.

REFEREE—Mr. J. LEWIS, BLACKBURN.   Kick-off 3·30 p.m.

ASTON VILLA.
Colours—Chocolate and Pale Blue.   GOAL.

T. Wilkes.

H. Spencer.   J. Welford.

J. Reynolds.   J. Cowan.   G. Russell.

C. Athersmith.   R. Chatt.   J. Devey.   D. Hodgetts.   S. Smith.

J. Banks.   T. Hutchinson.   Richards.   R. McLeod.   W. Bassett.

J. Taggart.   T. Higgins.   T. Perry.

W. Williams.   J. Horton.

J. Reader.

Colours—Blue and White.   GOAL.
WEST BROMWICH ALBION.

A record crowd of over 42,000 packed into the Crystal Palace ground to see the third FA Cup final meeting between Aston Villa and West Bromwich Albion in 1895. Villa had won in 1887 and Albion in 1892, and this time it was Villa who again came good on the day, winning 1-0 with a goal after just 39 seconds of play. It was scored by Bob Chatt with assistance from Albion 'keeper Bob Roberts and Jack Devey.

Caesar Jenkyns also played for Blues, serving the club religiously and efficiently in two spells between 1884 and 1896. During that time he scored 13 goals in 99 games. A Welsh international (8 caps) he was as tough as iron, feared no one and was a born leader, being controversial to the last. He was sent-off several times during a career that also saw him play for Manchester United and Walsall, the latter for five years from 1897.

Full-back Arthur Archer made 170 appearances for Birmingham between 1897 and 1902. An imposing figure, he was one of the toughest defenders in the game at that time and helped Blues gain promotion to the First Division in 1901. He later played for New Brompton, QPR, Norwich City, Brighton and Millwall.

These are the footballers who served the Saddlers a little over 100 years ago. From left to right (players only) back row: T. Bailey, T. Hawkins (goalkeeper), R. Smellie. Middle row: J.W. Davies, R. Cook, N. Forsyth. Front row: S. Holmes, W. McWhinnie, D. Copeland, S. Cox and J. O'Brien. The team finished tenth in the Second Division; Tom Bailey, Dick Cook, Norman Forysth, Sammy Holmes and Walter McWhinnie were the mainstays of the side, the latter top-scoring with 11 goals. David Copeland went on to play for Spurs and Chelsea.

Three years later it was all change and this was the Walsall team that started the 1897/98 season, having finished a disappointing twelfth in the Second Division in the previous campaign. From left to right, back row: G. Mountford (trainer), E. Hodson, J. Loynes, C.A. Jenkyns, C. Bunyan (goalkeeper), E. Peers, G. Johnson, J. Taggart, R. Ashwell (trainer). Front row: D. Horobin, J. Aston, S. Holmes, A. Wilkes, D. Copeland and A. Griffin. The Saddlers lifted themselves up two places this season, thanks mainly to the marksmanship of Jack Aston and George Johnson, who both netted 12 goals. Jack Taggart, ex-WBA and an Irish international, was an ever-present at left half while Albert Wilkes, who went on to play for Aston Villa and England, appeared in every game in the right half position. Prior to joining Walsall, Charlie Bunyan had conceded 26 goals when playing for Hyde against Preston North End in an FA Cup tie in October 1887. Caesar Jenkyns was the ex-Birmingham defender.

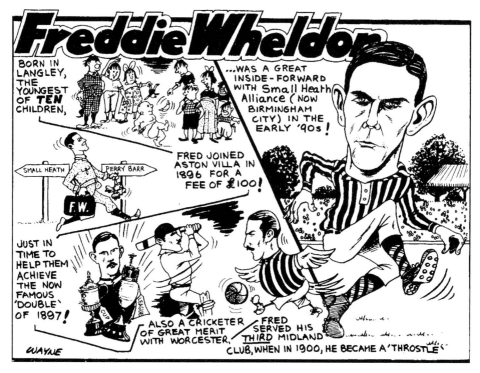

Wheldon was one of the Midlands' greatest sportsmen during the 1890s, serving with Aston Villa, Blues and Albion while scoring almost 5,000 runs for Worcestershire at an average of 22.54.

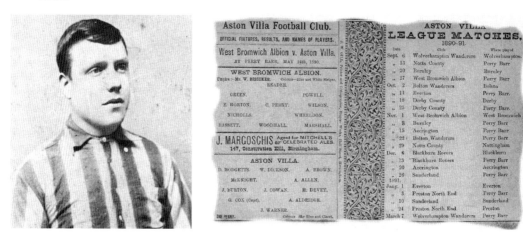

Above left: One of the first Scots to make the grade with Albion, Roddy McLeod was a skilful inside forward, who spent six years with the club from 1891. He drew up a terrific partnership with right-winger Billy Bassett and scored 65 goals in 185 games for Albion before transferring to Leicester Fosse. He was an FA Cup winner in 1892 and a runner-up in 1895, and later helped Brentford win the old Southern League Championship (1901).

Above right: A programme showing Wheldon (spelt Wheeldon here) in the Albion side as a trialist in a friendly match against his future club Aston Villa in May 1890. Villa won 1-0.

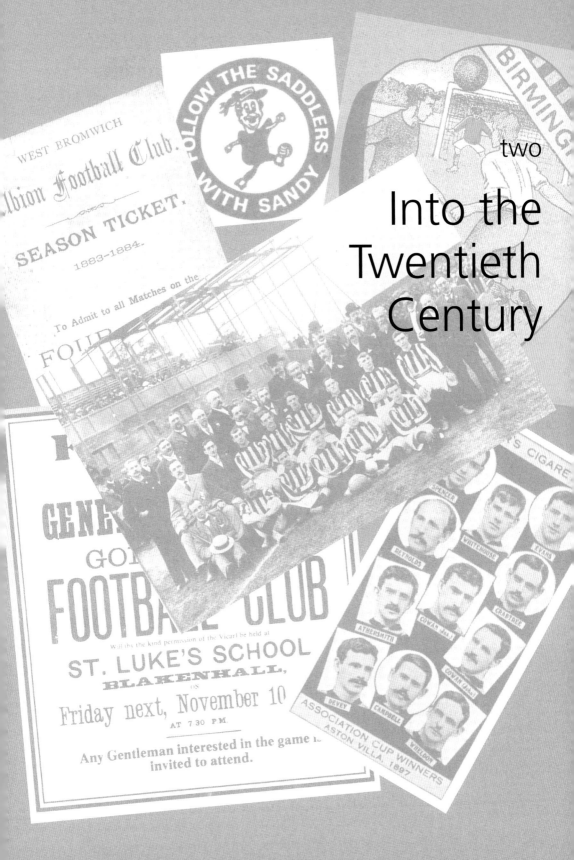

two

Into the Twentieth Century

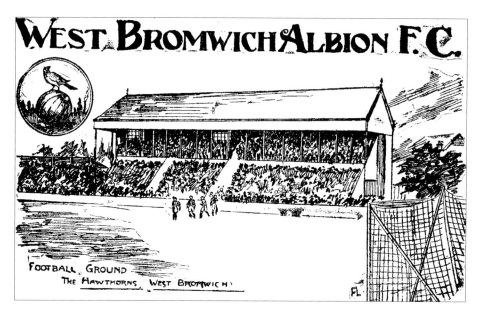

WEST BROMWICH ALBION F.C.

FOOTBALL GROUND
THE HAWTHORNS WEST BROMWICH

Caricature drawing of Albion's new ground, The Hawthorns, with the Halfords Lane stand prominent. The initial capacity was set at 35,000 and in 1935 it was said to be capable of housing around 65,000 spectators. Indeed, a record crowd of 64,815 packed inside to see the Baggies beat Arsenal 3-1 in a sixth round FA Cup tie in March 1937.

Above: Goalmouth action from the Birmingham *v.* Stoke League game at Muntz Street in April 1905. The visitors are under pressure as Blues attempt to grab an equaliser. They failed to crack open the Potters' defence and went down to a 1-0 defeat, losing by the same score at Stoke's Victoria ground a week later.

Right: Here is a very rare team-sheet issued for the first FA Cup tie staged at The Hawthorns, between West Bromwich Albion and Manchester City in February 1901. A crowd of 10,026 saw Ben Garfield's goal give Albion a 1-0 victory.

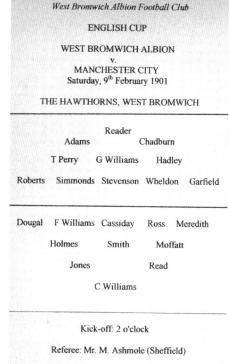

FOOTBALL !! FOOTBALL !! FOOTBALL !!

West Bromwich Albion Football Club

ENGLISH CUP

WEST BROMWICH ALBION
v.
MANCHESTER CITY
Saturday, 9th February 1901

THE HAWTHORNS, WEST BROMWICH

Reader

Adams   Chadburn

T Perry   G Williams   Hadley

Roberts Simmonds Stevenson Wheldon Garfield

Dougal F Williams Cassiday Ross Meredith

Holmes   Smith   Moffatt

Jones   Read

C Williams

Kick-off: 2 o'clock

Referee: Mr. M. Ashmole (Sheffield)

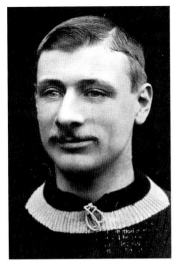

Alec Leake played in front of Spencer in that 1905 cup final, occupying the centre half position – where he also lined up for Birmingham and England. As skipper he appeared in 221 games for Blues in six years before going on to play in 140 games for Villa (1902-07). He later assisted Burnley. A genuine 'Brummagem Button', Leake won 5 caps and was actually named as an England reserve at the age of forty-one.

Howard Spencer skippered Villa in the 1905 FA Cup final. One of the great figures in English football, he was known as the 'Prince of Full-backs' and appeared in almost 300 games for the club between 1894 and 1907. He partnered Albert Evans when the double was won in 1897, was capped 6 times by England and, after retiring, was a director at Villa Park from 1909 until 1936.

In 1905, Aston Villa won the FA Cup for the fourth time, beating Newcastle United 2-0 at The Crystal Palace in front of a huge crowd of 101,117. Harry Hampton scored both goals, this being his first after just three minutes' play. En route to the final, Villa put out Leicester Fosse, Bury and Fulham (all at home) before disposing of Everton in the semi-final at Nottingham.

During the period 1903 to 1908, several League clubs switched from having single card programmes to a more substantial publication, comprising up to twelve pages. Aston Villa, West Bromwich Albion and Wolves issued their first official club matchday programmes around this time: Albion *v.* Burnley in September 1905, Villa *v.* Blackburn Rovers twelve months later and Wolves *v.* Bradford City in the FA Cup in January 1908. Pictured here is the front cover of the first *Villa News & Record* and also one from the Albion *v.* Chelsea from the same year. A crowd of 40,000 saw Villa beat Blackburn 4-2 while 25,500 saw Albion beaten 2-1 by Chelsea.

In December 1906 Birmingham moved from their Muntz Street ground to their present home at St Andrew's. A crowd of 32,000 saw the opening League game against Middlesbrough on Boxing Day, which ended goalless in freezing conditions. Most of the players in this picture were on the staff during that season (1906/07), when Blues took ninth position in the First Division, averaging 15,315 at their home games. The line-up shows, from left to right, back row: C. Simms (assistant trainer), O. Norman (trainer), J. Glover, A.C. Robinson, Mr W. Adams, F. Stokes, H. Howard, J. Dougherty, Dr Stanley, A. Jones (secretary). Front row: W.J. Beer, B. Green, A. Mounteney, W. Wigmore, W.H. Jones, F. Wilcox, C. Field. Benny Green had the pleasure of scoring the first goal at St Andrew's, in a 3-0 win over Preston North End on 29 December 1906.

At the end of the 1905/06 season Wolves – founder members of the Football League in 1888 – lost their First Division status, finishing bottom of the table with a dismal record of 8 wins and 23 defeats from their 38 matches played. They struggled from the word go and conceded 99 goals, scoring only 59. They also went out of the FA Cup in the second round, beaten by Bradford City 5-0, thus taking their goals-against tally for the season to 104. These are the players who performed rather indifferently for the Molineux club, from left to right, back row: A. Fletcher (trainer), T. Lunn (goalkeeper), E. Juggins, T. Baddeley (goalkeeper), J. Stanley, R. Betteley. Middle row: A. Baynham, J. Smith, W. Wooldridge, W. Layton, T. Raybould. On ground: E. James, H. Hughes, J. Whitehouse. Billy Wooldridge was the outstanding player, appearing in 33 League games and top-scoring with 12 goals.

Above left: Joe Pearson appeared in 118 first-class matches for Aston Villa between 1900 and 1908, gaining an FA Cup winner's medal in 1905 (after Villa had beaten Newcastle United 2-0). Born in the heart of the Black Country (in Bricrley Hill) he was a competent half-back who, after retiring, became a linesman, taking the flag for the England *v.* Scotland international at Villa Park in 1922. He was later Mayor of Stourbridge (1941-42).

Above right: Albert Evans was a sturdy, hard-tackling full-back who made 206 appearances for Aston Villa (1896-1907) before spending two seasons with West Bromwich Albion, later taking over as trainer at The Hawthorns. He gained three League Championship medals and in 1897 helped Villa complete the double. During his career Evans suffered five broken legs, three with Villa. He represented the Football League but missed out on a full England cap. He was ninety-two when he died in 1966.

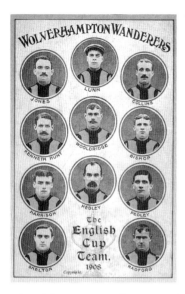  

JESSE PENNINGTON.
(West Bromwich Albion.)

Above left: In 1908 Wolves reached their third FA Cup final. They had won the first (in 1893 against Everton) and lost the second (1896 to Sheffield Wednesday). This time, as a Second Division club, they took on and defeated Newcastle United 3-1 at Crystal Palace in front of almost 75,000 spectators. En route to the final, Wolves knocked out Bradford City (in a replay), Bury, Swindon Town, Stoke and Southampton in that order. They played very well in the final; Billy Harrison, George Hedley and the Reverend Kenneth Hunt scoring the goals, while another 'H' – Jim Howie – replied for United. Right-winger Harrison, incidentally, became the father of triplets just before kick-off.

Above centre: Jesse Pennington was, in his prime, one of the finest full-backs anywhere in the land. Born in West Bromwich, he served Albion for nineteen years (1903-22) and in that time appeared in almost 500 competitive matches, leading the Baggies to the Second Division Championship in 1911, the FA Cup final the following season and to the coveted Football League title in 1920. He also gained 25 full caps for England (1907-20), played for an England XI on 5 occasions, represented the Football League 9 times, starred in 5 international trials and skippered both his club and country. In 1913 he was the subject of a bribe when a man offered him money to fix a game between Albion and Everton. 'Peerless' Pennington informed the Albion directors and the briber was later arrested and sentenced to six months in gaol at Stafford Assize Court.

Above right: Billy Garraty also represented England, gaining a full cap against Wales in 1903. A wonderfully-gifted goalscoring inside or centre forward, he played for Aston Villa, Leicester Fosse, Albion and Lincoln City between 1897 and 1911, netting over 125 goals in more than 300 career appearances. He was a League Championship and FA Cup winner with Villa in 1900 and 1905 respectively. After hanging up his boots, he became a delivery driver for Ansells brewery, Aston.

In season 1909/10, Walsall – out of the Football League, having lost their status eight years earlier – finished fifth in the Birmingham League, their highest placing in that competition at the time. They produced several outstanding displays and among their victories were those of 7-0 v. Halesowen, 4-0 v. Shrewsbury Town, 4-2 and 4-3 v. Stourbridge and 3-0 v. Dudley and West Bromwich Albion's reserve side. Billy Caddick top-scored with 18 goals, followed by Jack Crump with 16 and Bill Lyon with 10. (The trophies seen in this picture were won in local Cup competitions and Charity events.)

Tottenham Hotspur gained entry to the Football League in 1908 and they first opposed West Bromwich Albion at this level in November of that year, losing 3-0 at The Hawthorns and 3-1 at White Hart Lane. At the time Albion were striving to get out of the Second Division, but Spurs got over those two defeats to gain promotion to the top flight at the first attempt. Albion joined them for the 1911/12 season and travelled to London for a League game on 9 September. A crowd of 31,100 saw Spurs win 1-0. This picture shows the Albion goalkeeper Hubert Pearson punching clear from a Spurs corner with full-backs Jesse Pennington and Joe Smith on the line. Later in the season (mid-March) Albion gained revenge by winning the return fixture at The Hawthorns, 2-0.

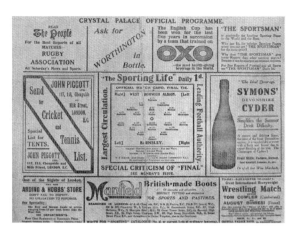

In 1912 Albion, the bookies' favourites, met Barnsley in the FA Cup final at Crystal Palace. A crowd of 55,213 saw a tough contest end goalless. The midweek replay was staged at Bramall Lane, Sheffield – not too far away from Barnsley, much to the annoyance of the Albion directors. This time, with 38,555 fans present (most of them supporting Barnsley), the Tykes snatched a dramatic last-minute goal at the end of extra-time to take the trophy from under Albion's noses. Jesse Pennington admitted that he should have 'fouled' Harry Tufnell, the Barnsley forward who broke clear and scored. But JP, the gentleman he was, simply could not commit a deliberate infringement of the rules and this act probably cost the Albion captain an FA Cup winner's medal. This is the programme from the first game of that 1912 cup final at Crystal Palace.

Joe Smith was a marvellously consistent full-back, born in Darby End, Dudley, who served West Bromwich Albion for sixteen years from 1910 and then had a spell with Birmingham. An England international, capped 3 times (twice at senior level), he made 471 first-class appearances for the Baggies, including 247 out of a possible 252 in the League between 1919 and 1925. In that six-year period he gained League Championship (1920) and runners-up medals (1925), having earlier helped the team win the Second Division title (1911). He was a tremendous partner to Jesse Pennington at The Hawthorns.

Dick Betteley, like Joe Smith, was a very useful, solid full-back, who made over 100 senior appearances for Wolves (from 1901) before spending six years at The Hawthorns, during which time he added a further 89 appearances to his tally. Born in Bilston, he helped Albion win the Second Division title in 1911 but, like Smith, unfortunately missed the 1912 FA Cup final. Betteley handed over the right-back position to Smith during the 1910/11 season.

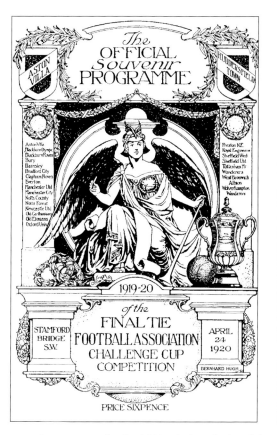

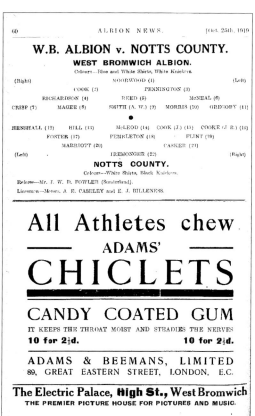

Programmes for the 1920 FA Cup final and for Albion's home game with Notts County. The year 1920 was an exceptional one for two of the main football clubs in the West Midlands and for another it was a reasonable campaign. Aston Villa won the FA Cup for the sixth time, beating Huddersfield Town 1-0 in the final at Stamford Bridge, Billy Kirton's 97th-minute deflected goal separating the teams. This was the first final to go into extra-time in the first game.

West Bromwich Albion, for the first (and so far only) time in the club's history, won the First Division title, recording 28 wins, notching up 60 points and scoring 104 goals. Their best win was a thumping 8-0 victory at home to Notts County, when Fred Morris scored five times.

Birmingham finished third in the Second Division, slotting in behind Tottenham Hotspur and Huddersfield – but they were to succeed the following year, going up as Champions. The Baggies' centre half Sid Bowser scored a hat-trick from that position in a 4-1 home win over Bradford City; nine players appeared in 34 or more League games, with only England international left half Bobby McNeal an ever-present and in the end Albion had nine points to spare over runners-up Burnley.

Fred Morris was born in Great Bridge and played for Albion before, during and after the Second World War. He joined the club from Redditch in 1911 and left for Coventry City in 1924, having scored 118 goals in 287 first-class matches, including a (then) club record 37 in the Championship-winning season of 1919/20. Strong, courageous with great anticipation, he was capped twice by England, represented both the FA and the Football League and in 1922 became the first Albion player to reach the century mark in League goals. He was the club's top-scorer in 1914/15, 1919/20 and 1920/21. A wonderful marksman, he was certainly one of the best of his time.

Dicky Baugh's father, also named Dicky, played as a full-back for Wolves in three FA Cup finals and twice for England. Baugh junior (pictured left) was also a fine full-back, who spent six years at Molineux from 1918 to 1924 when he was transferred to West Bromwich Albion, after a move to Cardiff City had fallen through. Quick off the mark, resilient with a timely tackle, he made 120 appearances for Wolves and 65 for the Baggies.

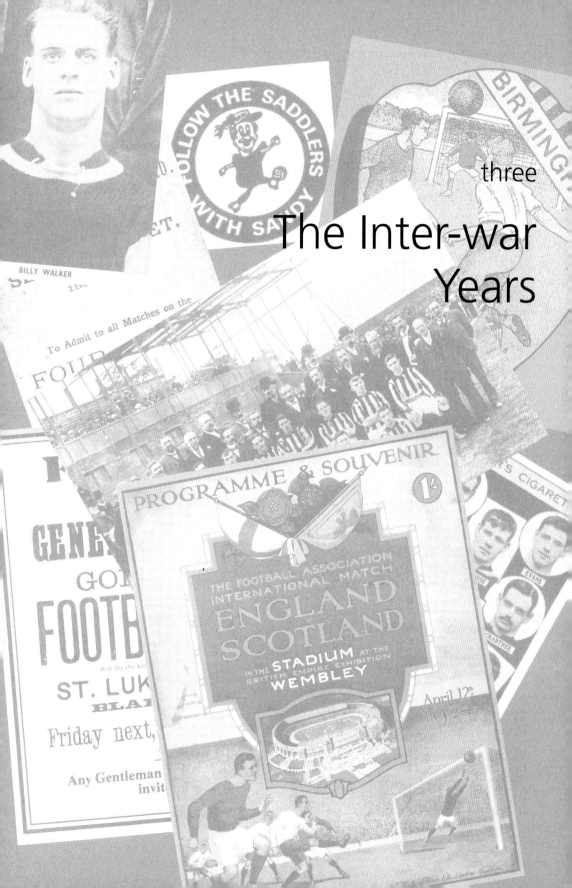

three

The Inter-war Years

G. GETGOOD

STAN. DAVIES.

Above left: Harry Hampton (left) and Johnny Crosbie played together in Birmingham's Second Division Championship-winning side of 1920/21. Between them they scored 30 goals, while fellow front man Jack Lane notched 15. Hampton, known as the 'Wellington Whirlwind' and 'Appy Arry' was a rampaging centre forward who loved to charge into goalkeepers. He had earlier rattled the net no fewer than 242 times in 373 games for Aston Villa before transferring across the city to St Andrew's in February 1920 after sixteen years at Villa Park. Twice an FA Cup winner (1905 and 1913) and a League Championship winner (1910), he gained four England caps and hit 31 goals in 59 games for Blues. Crosbie, a wonderful close dribbler, was the mastermind of the Blues' attack. He served the club from 1920 to 1932 and scored 72 goals in 432 senior matches. Signed from Ayr United for just £3,000, he won 2 Scottish caps and played in a Victory international in 1919. He was on the losing side in the 1931 FA Cup final *v.* West Bromwich Albion and after leaving Blues played briefly for Chesterfield.

Above centre: George Getgood was known affectionately as 'Goodman' – but he was far from that on the field, often putting in some crunching tackles from his wing half position. He played for Ayr United and Reading before joining Birmingham in 1922. After leaving St Andrew's he assisted Southampton, Wolves, Kidderminster Harriers, Aberdare and Shrewsbury Town. He helped Wolves win the Third Division (North) title in 1924 and during his career made well over 200 club appearances, but only 10 for Blues and 59 for Wolves.

Above right: Stan Davies was a versatile Welsh international who represented his country on 19 occasions, occupying six different positions. Big and strong, he preferred to play in the forward-line, where he performed admirably for both West Bromwich Albion (1921-27) and Birmingham (1927-28). He scored 83 goals in 159 games for the Baggies and 5 in 17 outings for Blues. He also played for Rochdale, Preston North End, Everton, Cardiff City, Rotherham and Barnsley and was awarded the Military Medal and the Croix de Guerre after distinguished service with the Welsh Fusiliers during the First World War.

During the inter-war years the Midlands were blessed with some exceptionally fine goalkeepers – here are three of them. *Top left:* Harry 'Shorty' Hibbs was a wonderfully consistent goalkeeper who made 388 appearances for Birmingham between 1926 and 1939. He was born in Tamworth and began as a centre forward, but after switching to stopping goals rather than scoring them, he became one of England's finest 'keepers, winning 25 caps and playing for Blues in their 1931 FA Cup final defeat by West Bromwich Albion. He later managed Walsall (1944-51). *Top right:* Harold Pearson was Harry Hibbs' cousin and kept goal for Albion against Blues in that 1931 cup Ffnal. Known as 'Algy', he was also born in Tamworth and joined the junior ranks at The Hawthorns in 1925 when his father, Hubert (also a goalkeeper), was still a registered player. Harold appeared in 303 senior games for the Baggies up to 1937, when he moved to Millwall. He played in the 1935 FA Cup final defeat by Sheffield Wednesday and gained a full England cap (*v.* Scotland at Wembley in 1932). *Above:* Noel George, acrobatic and courageous with a good temperament, was first choice between the posts for Wolves from 1921 to 1927, making 242 appearances and helping the Wanderers win the Third Division (North) title in 1924, conceding only 31 goals in 42 games. A native of Lichfield, he played for a Salonika XI against an Italian XI in 1919 and his display prompted Wolves to secure his services. Sadly, he was taken ill during his last game for the Molineux club (*v.* Bristol City) and, after being diagnosed with a terminal illness, died in his sleep at his home in Lichfield in October 1929, aged thirty-two.

| No.21 | No.6 | No.3 | No.17 |
| TEDDY BOWEN | ARTHUR BUTTERY | HAROLD SHAW | BILLY 'Knocky' WALKER |

These four players were all born in Hednesford and played for Hednesford Town before commencing their senior careers.

Teddy Bowen also played for Aston Villa for eleven years (1923-34) during which time he made almost 200 first-class appearances as a determined full-back. He moved to Norwich City from Villa Park and retired in 1938.

Arthur Buttery, an inside forward, scored 6 goals in 10 games for Wolves between 1929 and 1932. He had trials with both Motherwell and Swansea Town before arriving at Molineux. He later played for Bury, Bradford City, Walsall (1938-39) and Bristol Rovers.

Harold Shaw, a superb full-back, joined Wolves in 1923. He quickly helped them win the Third Division (North) title and went on to make 249 first-team appearances before moving to Sunderland for £7,000 in 1930. A League Championship winner with the Wearsiders in 1936, he retired after 217 games for the Roker Park club and thereafter concentrated on his golf at Penn, Wolverhampton.

Billy Walker scored 244 goals in 531 outings for Aston Villa (1919-33) when he retired to become manager of Sheffield Wednesday, later taking charge of Nottingham Forest. An inside left, capped 22 times by England, he was an FA Cup winner in 1920 and added two more medals to his collection when guiding both Wednesday and Forest to Wembley glory in 1935 and 1959 respectively.

Opposite below: In 1927/28, Walsall, based in the Third Division (South), finished a very disappointing eighteenth in the table, having transferred from the Northern section at the end of the previous campaign. 'A lot of work has to be done' said one director and in the summer of 1928 the Saddlers appointed Jim Kerr (ex-Coventry City) as their new manager in succession to Jimmy Torrance. Things improved slightly on the pitch and in Kerr's first season in charge Walsall moved up four places in the table (but were still nowhere near being promotion material). These are the players and officials of the club in 1928/29.

Above left: Mr George Fellows, a director of the club, was the man responsible for changing the name of Walsall's ground from Hilary Street to Fellows Park in 1930. The Saddlers remained at this ground until 1990, when they switched to their present home, the Bescot Stadium.

Above right: A typical Walsall matchday programme from March 1926, when the Saddlers were held to a goal-less draw at Fellows Park by Lincoln City.

In 1930/31 West Bromwich Albion completed what is still a unique double – winning the FA Cup and gaining promotion from the Second Division in the same season. Fielding a team made up entirely of English-born players, the Baggies brushed aside almost all before them as they raced on towards Wembley where they would meet and beat Midland rivals Birmingham 2-1 in the cup final, 'W.G.' Richardson scoring both goals (the second coming after Joe Bradford had equalised). And it was Richardson who top-scored in the League, netting 18 goals as Albion took the runners-up spot behind Everton to regain their top-flight status after a break of four years.

Tommy Glidden was Albion's skipper during that season and here he is seen shaking hands with his Blues counterpart Ned Barkas before the start of the FA Cup final. Glidden served Albion as a player, coach and director for some fifty years. An outside right, he joined the club in 1922 and scored 140 goals in 479 games before retiring in 1936, having played in the 1935 cup final defeat by Sheffield Wednesday. He was a club director from 1951 to 1974.

The victorious Albion team show off the FA Cup in 1931 when HRH the Prince of Wales (later King Edward VIII), standing next to club chairman Billy Bassett in the centre of the picture, visited The Hawthorns to congratulate the team on achieving their double success.

This is the beaten Blues side from that 1931 FA Cup final at Wembley. From left to right, back row: Mr A.L. Knighton (manager), J. Crosbie, G.R. Morrall, H. Hibbs, A. Leslie, E. Curtis, Mr A. Taylor (trainer). Front row: J.A. Cringan, G.R. Briggs, J. Bradford, E. Barkas, J. Firth, R. Gregg. On ground: G. Liddell, W. Horsman. En-route to their first final, Blues accounted for Liverpool, Port Vale, Watford, Chelsea and Sunderland.

Albion's match-winner at Wembley in 1931 was their ginger-haired, centre forward 'W.G.' Richardson, pictured in an unfamiliar hooped shirt (hands on knees), behind a colleague in a team line-up during the Second World War. Born in County Durham in 1909, he played for Hartlepool United immediately before joining Albion for what was to prove a bargain fee of just £1,250 in 1928. He scored on his Baggies' debut a year later (in a resounding 6-1 win over Millwall) and after that was awesome in front of goal. He got better and better and proceeded to bang home no fewer than 328 goals in 444 first-team games for the club up to 1945, when he moved to Shrewsbury Town. He netted four times in five minutes early in the League game at West Ham in November 1931, struck three goals in six minutes against Derby County two years later and in 1935/36 set a club record of 40 League and cup goals in a season. He was capped once by England (v. Holland) in 1935, the year he also played in his second cup final. After his spell at Gay Meadow 'W.G.' returned to The Hawthorns as trainer-coach and he was still playing the game he loved in 1959 when he collapsed and died in a charity match at Perry Barr. He was given the initials 'W.G.' to distinguish him from another W. Richardson who was with Albion at the same time.

Above: Albion recommenced their League battles with beaten FA Cup finalists Birmingham in the top flight of English football on Christmas Day 1931 and, in front of a Hawthorns' crowd of more than 38,000, the Blues gained sweet revenge for that Wembley defeat by recording a 1-0 victory. Here, Blues' goalkeeper Harry Hibbs watches the ball hit the side-netting with Albion's Joe Carter close at hand.

Opposite: In 1931/32 Wolves won the Second Division and so returned to the top flight of League football after an absence of twenty-six years. They played very well throughout the campaign, but in the end had only two points to spare over runners-up Leeds United with Stoke City third and Plymouth Argyle fourth. Under manager Major Frank Buckley, the Wanderers won 24 of their 42 matches and scored 115 goals while amassing 56 points. They thrashed Manchester United 7-0, Oldham Athletic 7-1, Chesterfield 6-0, Bury 6-0, Bradford 6-0, Millwall 5-0 and Southampton 5-1 at home and crushed Port Vale 7-1 in the Potteries. Billy Hartill top-scored with 30 goals and a total of twenty-two players were utilised by Buckley. Here are some of those players who helped bring top flight football back to Molineux, with a handful of reserves as well. From left to right, top row: John Griffiths, Percy Whittaker (goalkeeper), Cecil Shaw. Second row: Arthur Buttery, Albert Lumberg, Jack Smith. Third row: George Holley (trainer), George Bellis, Jack Bradford (assistant trainer). Front row: Leslie Redfern, David 'Boy' Martin and Mark Crook. Full-back Shaw later joined Albion (in 1937) and so did Smith, the latter as team manager in 1946, remaining in office until 1952.

Above left: In 1933 Walsall caused a major shock in the world of football when they knocked mighty Arsenal out of the FA Cup, shooting down the Gunners 2-0 in a third round tie at Fellows Park. A crowd of 11,149 saw Gilbert Alsop and Bill Sheppard (penalty) score the goals. In the next round the Saddlers lost 4-0 at Manchester City, when the attendance topped 52,000. This is the official programme from that epic encounter.

Above right: Centre half Reg Hollingsworth made 180 appearances for Wolves over a four-year period from 1928. He had started out with Mansfield Town and was in line for an England cap when he suffered a serious knee injury at Barnsley in March 1932. After retiring he joined the Staffordshire County police force and, in later years, worked at the Goodyear tyre factory in Wolverhampton. His death was somewhat tragic, suffering a heart attack while driving his car through Birmingham in 1969. He was fifty-nine.

Over the years there have been some cracking matches involving West Bromwich Albion and Wolves, both teams registering some impressive victories. One of Albion's biggest triumphs over their foes from Molineux was achieved in February 1935 when they won 5-2 in a League game at The Hawthorns – despite a solid display by young Stan Cullis in the Wolves' half-back line. This is a cartoon depiction of that local derby from almost seventy years ago.

In 1935 West Bromwich Albion returned to Wembley for their eighth appearance in an FA Cup final. Their opponents on this occasion were Sheffield Wednesday, a tough-tackling, well-built Yorkshire side, managed by the former Aston Villa star forward Billy Walker. Albion, who had won the trophy four years earlier, fielded nine players from that team, Jimmy Murphy and Walter Boyes replacing Tommy Magee and Stan Wood. Baggies' skipper Tommy Glidden and co-forward Joe Carter were struggling with injuries, but both declared themselves fit to play. They shouldn't have done (Jack Sankey and Arthur Gale were in form and ready to play). Wednesday won the game 4-2, scoring twice in the dying minutes after Teddy Sandford and Boyes had twice equalised for the Baggies. The picture shows Glidden tossing up for choice of ends with Ronnie Starling, the Owls' captain, before the start of the 1935 cup final (which, in fact, is the only one so far to be stopped by fog – being halted by the referee whose name was Arthur Fogg!).

Left: A cartoon depiction of the 1935 final.

Below: Match day ticket from the 1935 FA Cup final.

Above left: Gilbert Alsop was a Walsall legend – a goalscorer supreme who found the net no fewer than 169 times in only 222 games. He served the Saddlers from 1931 to 1948, having a mini-break with Albion in the mid-1930s (one game). He also played for Coventry City and, after retiring, became groundsman at Fellows Park, a job he held for many years up to 1970. He was eighty-three when he died.

Above centre: Eric Houghton served Aston Villa for a total of forty-six years. Mainly a winger with one of the strongest shots in the game, he scored 258 goals in 547 appearances for Villa (170 goals in 390 League and cup games) between 1927 and 1946 when he moved to Notts County. He returned as Villa's manager in 1953 and four years later guided them to FA Cup final glory over Manchester United. He became a director at Walsall and, after a coaching appointment with Villa, was voted onto the board in 1972, later taking office as vice-president until his death in 1996. Capped 7 times by England, he helped Villa win the Wartime North Cup in 1944.

Above right: Dennis Westcott, like Alsop, was a terrific centre forward. He scored 215 goals in 230 matches for Wolves between 1937 and 1948, including 91 in only 76 wartime fixtures. Born on Merseyside, he had trials with West Ham and served with New Brighton before moving to Molineux. After leaving Wolves he signed for Blackburn and later assisted Manchester City, Chesterfield and Stafford Rangers. Unlucky not to have won a full England cap, Westcott played in 4 Victory internationals and in Wolves' 1939 FA Cup final defeat by Leicester City, having netted four goals in the semi-final against Grimsby (when a record crowd of almost 77,000 packed into Old Trafford). In 1942 he helped Wolves win the Wartime League (North) Cup, scoring in both legs of the final against Sunderland.

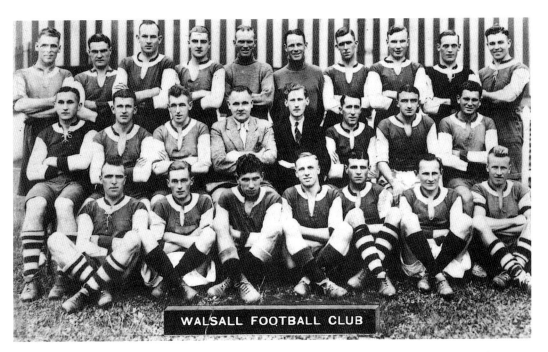

WALSALL FOOTBALL CLUB

In 1936/37, Walsall claimed seventeenth place in the Third Division (South) and reached the fourth round of the FA Cup. They only occasionally produced a useful display, mainly at home, with wins over Bristol Rovers (5-2), Swindon Town (5-2), and Exeter City (4-2) the best. They lost 5-1 at Bristol City, 6-3 at Northampton and drew 4-4 with Aldershot. With Alsop away with Albion, Bill Evans top-scored with 15 goals, followed Len Dunderdale with 10. Here is the Walsall squad from the 1936/37 campaign.

In 1937/38, Wolverhampton Wanderers came mighty close to winning their first League Championship, finishing as runners-up. Major Frank Buckley had assembled a fine side that included goalkeeper Alex Scott, full-backs Bill Morris and John Taylor, half-backs Stan Cullis and Joe Gardiner and forwards Teddy Maguire, Tom Galley, Dennis Westcott, Bryn Jones (soon to move to Arsenal for a record fee) and George Ashall. Westcott (19 goals) was top-scorer while Dicky Dorsett was also getting into his stride – bagging four with Westcott when hapless Leicester City were hammered 10-1 at Molineux. These are the signatures of the Wolves players from that excellent season.

Above left: Bob Iverson played for Tottenham Hotspur and Lincoln City, among others, before joining Wolves at the age of twenty-four in 1935. A big, strong honest defender, he scored 7 goals in 37 games during his time at Molineux, which ended in December 1936, when he moved to Aston Villa. He spent the next twelve years wearing the claret-and-blue strip, playing in over 325 matches (173 during the Second World War) and gaining a Second Division Championship and Wartime League (North) Cup winner's medals in 1938 and 1944 respectively. Iverson, a keen angler and self-taught pianist, who also loved jazz, died in 1953.

Above right: Full-back Bill Morris was an amateur, playing in West Bromwich Albion's Colts team before slipping through The Hawthorns net. A few years later, in 1933, he signed professional forms for Wolves and went on to appear in more than 260 competitive games for the club, including 68 appearances during the war. He was a member of Wolves' beaten 1939 FA Cup final side and in that same season won 3 caps for England, taking the field against Ireland, Scotland and Romania, finishing up on the winning side each time. He ended his career with Dudley Town.

Above, from left to right:

In August 1938, inside forward Bryn Jones moved from Wolves to Arsenal for a then record transfer fee of £14,000. He had scored 57 goals in 177 appearances during his time at Molineux and later played in 74 first-class matches for the Gunners. A Welsh international, he was capped 17 times at senior level and on 8 occasions during the war.

Stan Cullis served Wolves for thirty years. He signed professional forms as a player in 1934 and left Molineux in 1964, having managed the side since 1948. A defender of the highest class, he made almost 200 appearances (24 during the Second World War) and was skipper for the 1939 FA Cup final. As manager he guided Wolves to three League titles (1954, 1958 and 1959) and two FA Cup final triumphs (1949 and 1960). He was later in charge of Birmingham City (1964-68).

During the 1930s, Dai Richards played for three West Midland clubs – Wolves, Birmingham and Walsall – and he also assisted Merthyr Town (1925-27) and Brentford, plus a handful of non-League sides. A Welsh international wing half (21 caps) he was a fine passer of the ball and during his career accumulated over 350 senior appearances for clubs and country: 229 as a Wolves player, whom he helped win the Second Division Championship in 1932.

Owing to the form of Alex Scott and then Bert Williams, goalkeeper Cyril Sidlow made only 4 League appearances for Wolves (plus another 92 during the war) between 1937 and 1946. Thereafter he gave Liverpool excellent service, playing in over 150 senior games, including an outing in the 1950 FA Cup final (*v.* Arsenal). A Welsh international, capped 11 times in wartime football (he played against England at The Hawthorns in 1945 when Bert Williams was on the opposite side), Sidlow later assisted New Brighton. Born in 1915, he is now one of the oldest surviving Wolves players, and lives in Codsall.

ASTON VILLA FOOTBALL CLUB

TOUR IN GERMANY
MAY, 1938

ITINERARY

Above left: Don Dearson (Blues) firing in a shot at the Albion goal during the League game at St Andrew's on 15 April 1938. The two Albion defenders, arms raised, are Bob Finch (left) and Harry Lowery. After seven years in the First Division, West Bromwich Albion were relegated at the end of the 1937/38 season. With no fewer than twelve teams all in trouble, they had everything to play for come Easter after drawing with Arsenal and beating Brentford. Indeed, they were confident of avoiding the drop at that stage of the campaign but a disappointing 2-1 defeat against fellow strugglers Birmingham at St Andrew's and a 7-1 hammering at bottom club Manchester City seemed to have knocked the stuffing out of the team. However, the Baggies bounced back immediately with successive home wins over Blues (4-3) and Huddersfield Town (5-1) and almost certainly only needed three points from their remaining three matches to retain their top flight status. They couldn't manage one – losing to Blackpool, Wolves and Middlesbrough to fall through the trapdoor in bottom spot on 36 points. Manchester City (who scored 80 goals, more than the Champions Arsenal) slipped out of the division with them (38 pts) while Grimsby Town, Portsmouth, Birmingham and Stoke City all survived, each having also chalked up 38 points.

Above right: At the end of the 1937/38 season, with war looming, Aston Villa went on a tour to Germany. They played three matches – beating an Austrian-orientated German 'Select' XI 3-2 in Berlin, lost 2-1 to a Greater German XI in Dusseldorf and defeated a strong German XI 2-1 in Stuttgart. Prior to the opening game in the Olympic Stadium, the Villa boss Jimmy Hogan received a particularly warm welcome as he had previously managed the Austrian national team, while his players declined to give the Nazi salute with 110,000 spectators looking on in sweltering 90 degrees heat. This is the official itinerary issued by the club prior to that German tour in 1938.

Above left: In 1939, Wolves, the favourites, played relegation-threatened Portsmouth in the FA Cup final at Wembley. A crowd of 99,370 attended the contest which ended in a surprise 4–1 victory for Pompey as Wolves froze on the day. In fact, it turned out to be a rather one-sided match. Portsmouth took a deserved lead on 30 minutes through ex-Wolves player Bert Barlow. Anderson made it 2-0 just before half-time before Barlow struck again 45 seconds after the restart. Dicky Dorsett reduced the deficit on 65 minutes but Parker rubbed salt into Wolves' wounds with his side's fourth goal with 18 minutes remaining. This is the beaten Wolves side of 1939, from left to right, back row: T. Galley, W. Morris, S. Cullis, A. Scott, F. Taylor, J. Gardiner. Front row: S. Burton, A. McIntosh, D. Westcott, R. Dorsett and E. Maguire.

Above centre: Frank Broome was a wonderfully-gifted forward who scored 92 goals in 138 competitive games for Aston Villa between 1934 and 1946. He also played for Derby County, Notts County, Brentford and Crewe, won 10 England caps (7 at senior level) and, after retiring, managed Notts County, Exeter City and Southend United. He was a Second Division title winner with Villa (1938), helped Wolves win the Wartime League (North) Cup as a guest in 1942 and was a member of Crewe's Third Division (South) Championship-winning side in 1950.

Above right: Ernie 'Mush' Callaghan was a tough, uncompromising defender who made 142 peacetime appearances for Aston Villa whom he served for seventeen years (1930-47). With Broome, he helped them win the Second Division title in 1938 and later collected a Wartime League Cup (North) winner's medal when Blackpool were defeated in the two-legged final in 1944. Born in Birmingham in 1910, he played initially for Hinckley Athletic and then Atherstone Town, and after retiring became the odd-job man around Villa Park. He received a testimonial before his death in 1972.

Below left: Serving their country during the Second World War – footballers Billy Wright (Wolves, left), Neil Franklin (Stoke City, centre) and Harry Kinsell (West Bromwich Albion) all represented England in Victory internationals during the 1945/46 transitional season. Wright became a household name at Molineux; Franklin was a star performer at the heart of the Potters' defence and Kinsell, who also played for West Ham United and Bolton Wanderers, was a tough-tackling left-back who helped the Baggies gain promotion from the Second Division in 1949.

Below right: Ken Davies was a nippy outside right whose career was severely interrupted by war. He started out with Wolves in 1943, scored twice in two outings, and then moved to Walsall in 1946, allowing fellow winger Johnny Hancocks to move to Molineux. He later assisted Brighton & Hove Albion.

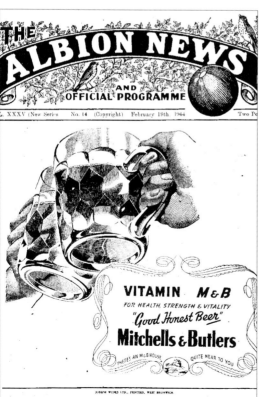

Left: On 19 February 1944, West Bromwich Albion met Stoke City in a Wartime League Cup tie at The Hawthorns. The 5,000 crowd anticipated a close game, as the Baggies had lost only one of their previous six matches while the Potters had suffered defeat just once in their last eight. What happened on the pitch was quite amazing... Stoke won 8-2 (Freddie Steele scoring four times and Tommy Sale three) as Albion's defence collapsed under pressure and the team suffered its heaviest home defeat during the Second World War. A week later the teams met at The Victoria Ground and this time, despite a Billy Elliott hat-trick for the Baggies, Stoke won 5-4 to complete a quick double. This is the programme produced for the ten-goal encounter at The Hawthorns.

four

Into the Fifties

Above, from left to right:

Jesse Pye was a record £12,000 signing by Wolves from Notts County in 1946. He replaced Dennis Westcott as leader of the attack and went on to score 95 goals, including two in the 1949 FA Cup final win over Leicester City, in 209 games before transferring to Luton Town in 1952. An England international, he later served with Derby County.

Jack Vernon spent five years with West Bromwich Albion (1947-52) appearing in 200 games and scoring one goal – the winner against Sheffield Wednesday on Christmas Day 1948. A brilliant centre half, he won 22 caps for Northern Ireland and Eire, represented Great Britain *v.* The Rest of Europe and played for the United Kingdom *v.* Wales.

This is the programme from the match when West Bromwich Albion claimed their biggest post-war away win in Second Division football: 7-2 over Newport County in September 1946. That afternoon, in front of 20,521 fans, Tipton-born striker Ike Clarke scored four times. Later in the season, the Welsh side drew 2-2 at The Hawthorns.

West Bromwich-born wing half Gil Williams had few opportunities with the Albion, appearing in 37 first-team matches, 28 during the Second World War. He did, however, take part in a fourth round FA Cup tie against Spurs at White Hart Lane when a crowd of 71,853 – the biggest to watch Albion in this competition apart from a final – saw the Londoners win 3-1.

Opposite: Billy Wright, seen here shaking hands with the Leicester City skipper Norman Plummer before Wolves' 3-1 FA Cup final victory in 1949, appeared in over 650 games for the Molineux club (490 at League level) during a playing career that covered twenty-one years (1938-59). He was a recipient of three League Championship medals (1954, 1958 and 1959) and won 105 caps for England, leading his country on 70 occasions. After retiring, he managed the nation's Under-23 side and also Arsenal (1962-66) and later returned to Molineux as a director in 1990. Awarded the OBE in 1959 and married to one of the famous Beverley sisters (Joy), he was one of Wolves' greatest ever players. He died at the age of seventy-two in 1996.

Right: Wright's 1949 FA Cup winning medal.

Left: The 1948/49 season was an exceptional one for Black Country football as Wolves won the FA Cup and Albion gained promotion from the Second Division after clawing back a huge points deficit to edge out Southampton and climb back into the top flight with the Champions Fulham. The picture shows captains Jack Vernon (Albion) and Billy Wright (Wolves) going through the preliminaries before the sixth round FA Cup-tie at Molineux in March 1949. A goal by Jimmy Mullen edged out the Baggies 1-0 as Wolves went on their way to Wembley.

WEST BROMWICH ALBION
FOOTBALL CLUB
WINNERS OF PROMOTION
TO FIRST DIVISION

1948-49

CELEBRATION
DINNER

HELD AT THE

GRAND HOTEL, BIRMINGHAM
WEDNESDAY, JULY 27TH, 1949

Above left: Dave Walsh who was capped 11 times by Ireland and on 20 occasions by Eire, played for three West Midlands clubs: West Bromwich Albion (1946-50), Aston Villa (1950-55) and Walsall (1955-56). A brilliant centre forward, he scored exactly 100 goals for the Baggies, helping them win promotion in 1949, and followed up by netting 40 for Villa and 9 for the Saddlers. He found the net in each of his first six Football League games for Albion at the start of the 1946/47 season (a record). Walsh now aged eighty-one, lives in Thurlestone, South Devon.

Above right: The official invitation to Albion's Celebration Dinner at the Grand Hotel, Birmingham after their promotion to the First Division in 1949.

In December 1948, Birmingham City met Wolves in a First Division fixture at St Andrew's and in front of a 48,000 crowd they went down 1-0, a Jesse Pye goal deciding a tight contest. Earlier in the season, more than 54,000 spectators had witnessed the 2-2 draw at Molineux – Blues' first game in the top flight since April 1939. The picture shows England goalkeeper Bert Williams preparing to gather a high ball off the head of Blues' left-winger Harry Roberts, with teammates Roy Pritchard (3) and Billy Wright close at hand.

Above, from left to right:

Some of the older Birmingham City supporters still say that Gil Merrick was a better goalkeeper than Harry Hibbs, although others see it differently. Whatever the case may be, Merrick gave the club excellent service for twenty-two years (1938-60), appearing in 551 first-class matches (still a record) and helping Blues twice win promotion from the Second Division and reach the FA Cup final in 1956. Then, as manager, he guided the team to an Inter-Cities Fairs Cup final (1961) and to League Cup glory (1963 *v*. Aston Villa). Capped 23 times by England, Merrick is now well into his eighties.

Peter Murphy scored 127 goals in 278 senior games for Blues whom he served from 1952 to 1961, having been an amateur at St Andrew's as a teenager. He made his League debut for Coventry City in 1946 and then helped both Tottenham Hotspur (1951) and Blues (1955) win the Second Division title. An FA Cup finalist in 1956, Murphy accidentally collided with the Manchester City goalkeeper Bert Trautmann, causing the German to break his neck. Murphy was fifty-three when he died in 1975.

Brierley Hill-born centre half Trevor Smith played for England schoolboys with Duncan Edwards and when Billy Wright retired from international duty in 1959, he starred in 2 full internationals (against Wales and Sweden). Strong and competitive, he made 430 first-class appearances for Blues over a period of thirteen years (1951-64), helping them win promotion in 1955 and reach the FA Cup final a year later. He also played in the Inter Cities Fairs Cup and League Cup finals of 1961 and 1963, gaining a winner's medal in the latter. He ended his professional career with Walsall.

Competitive full-back Ken 'Slasher' Green lies in fourth place in the list of Blues all-time appearance-makers. He played in 443 senior games for the club, whom he served between 1943 and 1959. A very consistent defender, he twice helped Blues gain promotion from the Second Division (1948 and 1955) and played in the 1956 FA Cup final defeat by Manchester City. Capped twice by England at 'B' team level, he twice represented the Football League and was truly a great servant at St Andrew's.

Jeff Hall was a marvellous footballer, being a right-back specialist whose career was sadly ended when he was struck down with polio and died at the age of twenty-nine. An amateur with Bradford Park Avenue, he joined the Blues as a professional in 1950 and went on to appear in 264 competitive games before falling ill in 1959. He helped win the Second Division Championship in 1955 and reach the FA Cup final a year later. Capped 17 times by England, he also represented his country at 'B' team level and played 4 times for the Football League side. Hall was without doubt one of the classiest full-backs ever to don a Blues shirt.

Above left: Full-back Roy Pritchard – a Wolves player from 1941 to 1956 – made 223 appearances for the club, gaining an FA Cup winner's medal in 1949 and a First Division Championship medal in 1954. During the Second World War he guested for Notts County, Mansfield Town, Swindon Town and Walsall and, on leaving Molineux, signed for Aston Villa, later assisting Notts County (again), Port Vale and Wellington Town.

Above centre: Inside forward Jimmy Dunn, the son of a former Everton and Scotland international, was an FA Cup winner with Wolves in 1949. He joined the groundstaff at Molineux in 1941 and scored 40 goals in 144 games for the club before transferring to Derby County in 1952, later assisting Worcester City and Runcorn. Dunn twice returned to Wembley as trainer of West Bromwich Albion.

Above right: Bert Williams was a great goalkeeper who played for Walsall, Wolves and England in a professional career spanning twenty years. He started out at Fellows Park in 1937, moved to Molineux in 1945 and retired in 1957 after making 420 appearances. Both an FA Cup and League Championship winner in 1949 and 1954 respectively, he was capped 24 times by his country and played in the 1950 World Cup.

Above left: Relaxing on the bowling green in 1952 – West Bromwich Albion manager/coach Jesse Carver (left), former Baggies player Harry Ashley, club physiotherapist Fred Pedley and ex-left-winger Arthur Fitton chasing the jack. Carver was a brilliant coach who assembled the great Albion side that finished as runners-up in the First Division and won the FA Cup in 1954. A former Blackburn Rovers, Newcastle United and Bury defender, he also coached in Italy at Lazio, AS Roma, Juventus, Inter Milan, Torino and Genoa, and was in charge of Coventry City in the mid-1950s. Ashley was basically a reserve at The Hawthorns, where he also acted as trainer and odd-job man. Pedley was later physiotherapist with Aston Villa and Fitton hit 11 goals in 99 games for Albion (1922-32) and later served with Manchester United, Preston and Coventry. He became a warden on Kinver Edge.

Above right: Ray Barlow was a long-striding wing half in Albion's brilliant side of the mid-1950s. He served the club from 1944 to 1960, making 482 appearances, scoring 48 goals. He also played at centre forward, inside left and centre half; was a promotion winner in 1949, an FA Cup winner five years later and gained one cap for England (1954 *v.* Ireland). He left the Hawthorns for Birmingham City and later ran a newsagents and tobacconists shop in Stourbridge. Barlow, born in 1926, now lives in Pedmore.

Right: Eddie Brown was an unorthodox centre forward who scored 90 goals in 185 games for Birmingham City between 1954 and 1959. He helped Blues win the Second Division Championship and reach the FA Cup final in successive years (1955 and 1956) and during a lengthy career he also played for Preston North End, Southampton, Coventry City, Leyton Orient, Scarborough, Stourbridge, Bedworth and Wigan Athletic. He retired to become a games teacher in his native Preston.

Clockwise from top left:

Three of Wolves' 1949 FA Cup and 1954 League Championship winning sides – outside left Jimmy Mullen (top), skipper Billy Wright and goalkeeper Bert Williams. All played for England and together they appeared in 1,447 senior games for Wolves with Mullen also netting 112 goals. Mullen had, in fact, made his debut for the club as a sixteen year-old in 1939.

Inside forward Peter Broadbent was also a League Championship winner with Wolves, collecting three medals (1954, 1958 and 1959). He helped the Wanderers win the FA Cup (1960), appeared in 497 first-class matches (145 goals) and gained 7 caps for England. He also played for Shrewsbury Town and Aston Villa.

Centre forward Roy Swinbourne (in action *v.* the Blues) thrived on the service of Broadbent and Mullen when Wolves took the League title in 1954. That season he scored 24 goals and all told netted 114 times (in 230 outings) for the Molineux club with whom he was a professional for nine years (1948-57). A knee injury forced him into early retirement.

In 1954 Wolves and Albion were involved in a ding-dong tussle to decide the League Championship. That honour eventually went to Molineux and the Baggies finished runners-up, but made up for this disappointment by lifting the FA Cup, beating Preston North End 3-2 in the final. These are the players who took Albion to Wembley. Sadly, goalkeeper Heath and right-back Rickaby both missed the final through injury. They were replaced by Jimmy Sanders and Joe Kennedy respectively.

Right: Left-back Len Millard, seen here collecting the FA Cup from HRH The Queen Mother after Albion had defeated Preston North End in the 1954 cup final, served the club for twenty-one years (1937-58), making 627 first-team appearances and scoring 18 goals, including a hat-trick against Wolves in a wartime game in 1942 when playing as a centre forward. He also helped Albion win the Midland War Cup (1944) and gain promotion from the Second Division five years later. wing half Jimmy Dudley (4) is picking up the plinth.

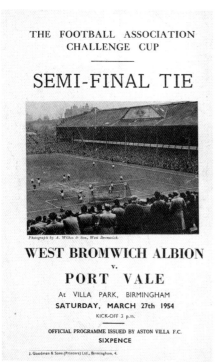

Above left: Programme from Albion's 1954 FA Cup final encounter with Port Vale at Villa Park. The Baggies won 2-1 with goals from Jimmy Dudley and Ronnie Allen, who netted a penalty against his former club.

Above right: You had to pay at least 3s 6d for a ticket to watch Albion in the FA Cup final in 1954. The attendance at Wembley was 99,852.

Left: At the end of the 1954/55 season Wolverhampton Wanderers accepted an invitation to tour the Soviet Union, taking on two of the best teams in Russia – Moscow Spartak and Moscow Dynamo. They lost both matches after spirited performances, but soon afterwards when Dynamo visited England, Wolves gained sweet revenge with a 2-1 victory under the Molineux floodlights, having thumped Spartak 4-0 on the same ground before travelling behind the Iron Curtain. The picture here shows action from Wolves' friendly encounter against Spartak in 1955.

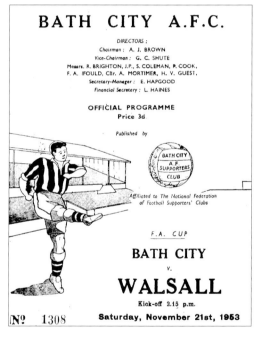

Above left: In 1953/54 Walsall faced non-League opposition in the FA Cup. They were drawn against Bath City from the Southern League and after a tough contest won through to the second round with a 3-0 scoreline, Norman Allsopp, George Dean and Fred Morris the scorers in front of 10,700 fans at Twerton Park, a ground later occupied by Bristol Rovers. This is the programme from that encounter, played over fifty years ago.

Above right: Tony Richards gave Walsall excellent service as a centre forward for nine years during which time he scored a club record (later bettered by Alan Buckley) 198 goals in 358 senior appearances – all this after being rejected by Birmingham City! He helped the Saddlers rise from the Fourth to the Second Division in double-quick time and in a poll carried out in the late 1990s, was voted Walsall's best-ever player.

Two years after West Bromwich Albion had represented the Midlands in the FA Cup final, Birmingham City met Manchester City in the final of the same competition in 1956. Having played all their ties away from home, including wins at The Hawthorns and Highbury plus victory over Sunderland in the semi-final, Blues were confident of success over their Maine Road opponents. Sadly, it was not to be as the team from Manchester won 3-1, despite their German-born goalkeeper Bert Trautmann fracturing his neck in a collision with Peter Murphy. Noel Kinsey netted Blues' consolation goal. This was Blues' second defeat in the final, having lost to neighbours WBA twenty-five years earlier. Here you see Trautmann diving at the feet of the Blues' centre forward Eddie Brown with centre half Dave Ewing giving support to his 'keeper.

THE FOOTBALL ASSOCIATION CHALLENGE CUP COMPETITION

FINAL TIE

BIRMINGHAM CITY
v
MANCHESTER CITY

SATURDAY, MAY 5th, 1956   KICK-OFF 3 pm

Left and below: Programme and ticket from that 1956 cup final.

EMPIRE STADIUM
WEMBLEY

Chairman and Managing Director   SIR ARTHUR J. ELVIN, MBE
OFFICIAL PROGRAMME   -   ONE SHILLING

EAST STANDING ENCLOSURE

ENTER AT TURNSTILES (See plan & conditions on back)   D
ENTRANCE   10

EMPIRE STADIUM, WEMBLEY
The Football Association
Cup Competition

FINAL TIE

SATURDAY, MAY 5th, 1956
KICK-OFF 3 p.m.

Price 3/6
(Including Tax)   Chairman & Managing Director
Wembley Stadium Limited

THIS PORTION TO BE RETAINED
This Ticket is issued on the condition that it is not re-sold for more than its face value

Top: This photograph shows West Bromwich Albion manager Vic Buckingham (extreme left) with his professional squad assembling at The Hawthorns for pre-season training in July 1957 (after a successful tour of Russia). The player at the back, above the rest, is Albion's 1954 FA Cup final hero Frank Griffin and on the extreme right is Joe Kennedy, who also played a big part in that success at Wembley.

Middle: Derek 'The Tank' Kevan was an Albion player for ten years (1953-63). In that time he scored 173 goals in 291 League and cup games and also netted 8 times in 14 full internationals for England, taking part in the World Cup finals in 1958. In an excellent career, he also played for Bradford Park Avenue (his first major club), Manchester City, Crystal Palace, Luton Town, Peterborough United, Stockport County, Macclesfield Town and Boston United. A hardened Yorkshireman and member of the Albion ex-players' association, he was born in Ripon in 1935 and now lives in retirement in Birmingham.

Bottom: Bobby Robson played with Kevan in Albion's team from 1956 to 1962. A wing half or inside forward, he hit 61 goals in 257 games for the Baggies and won 20 caps for England, scoring twice on his debut against France in 1957. He also played in the 1958 World Cup finals. Robson later served with Fulham (two spells) and managed the Cottagers, Ipswich Town and England, as well as being in charge of several European clubs, including FC Porto, PSV Eindhoven, Barcelona and Sporting Lisbon. Awarded the CBE in 1991, he was boss of Newcastle United from 1999 to 2004 and was knighted for services to football.

In 1957 Aston Villa became the fourth West Midlands club to reach the FA Cup final in eight years, following Wolves (1949), Albion (1954) and Birmingham City (1956). Villa's opponents were the double-seeking Busby Babes of Manchester United, who were red hot favourites to lift the trophy at Wembley. Villa were plucky to the last, however, and it was Eric Houghton's men who went on to triumph, Peter McParland (top right) netting both goals in a spirited 2-1 victory. Here is a copy of the programme from that final and Villa skipper Johnny Dixon hugging the FA Cup as he makes his way down the thirty-nine steps from Wembley's Royal Box.

An action picture of Allen scoring for Albion against Manchester City at The Hawthorns in February 1953, when a crowd of nearly 28,000 saw the Baggies win 2-1. Ronnie Allen was an Albion player from 1950 to 1961 and later returned to The Hawthorns as manager (two spells) and as a coach, spending more than twenty-five years at the club (in various capacities). A tremendous centre forward, he actually started as a right-winger with Port Vale before his £20,000 transfer to Albion, who converted him into 'leader of the attack' – and how well he performed wearing the number 9 shirt! An FA Cup winner in 1954 (when he scored twice in the final against Preston, including an equalising penalty) he netted 218 goals in 437 competitive games for the Baggies and was capped 5 times by England. He also played for Crystal Palace, was in charge of both Wolves and Walsall and coached/managed in the Far East, Greece and Spain. He was, in many respects 'The Complete Footballer'. Ronnie Allen died in June 2001, aged seventy-two.

Allen being denied by Arsenal goalkeeper Jack Kelsey.

In these days it is very rare for a football match to go ahead in icy conditions, even on a snowbound pitch. But in years gone by, the game and the players were tough and here you see Albion in action against Charlton Athletic at The Valley in 1956. The Albion players, from left to right, are Len Millard (captain), Don Howe (preparing to clear the ball), Ronnie Allen, Gerry Summers, goalkeeper Jimmy Sanders and Joe Kennedy (behind Charlton striker Stuart Leary). The game turned out to be a disaster for Albion, who crashed to a 5-1 defeat in front of 13,573 hardy spectators.

Above left: Dual-purpose winger Harry Hooper played for West Ham, Wolves (1956-57), Birmingham City (1957-60) and Sunderland and won England caps at 'B' and Under-23 levels. The son of an ex-Sheffield Wednesday defender of the same name, he made over 350 appearances in all and scored 120 goals, including 19 for Wolves and 42 for Blues.

Above right: Bill Guttridge, a rock-solid, uncompromising full-back who feared no-one, appeared in 6 League games for Wolves before going on to play in well over 200 competitive games for Walsall (1954-62), helping the Saddlers gain promotion to the Second Division (from the Fourth) in successive seasons.

In 1956/57 Walsall finished fifteenth in the Third Division (South) table, their equal–best placing since 1948/49. Albert McPherson was signed from Bury and made over 350 League appearances for the club. Harry Haddington, goalkeeper Reg Davies, Eric Perkins and Ken Hodgkisson all joined from West Bromwich Albion. Don Dorman was once a Birmingham City player and Sammy Moore was a junior with Wolves; 'Tot' Leverton played for both Nottingham clubs (Forest and County); Tom Brown was recruited from Ipswich Town and Doug Taylor was an amateur at The Hawthorns and a reserve at Molineux.

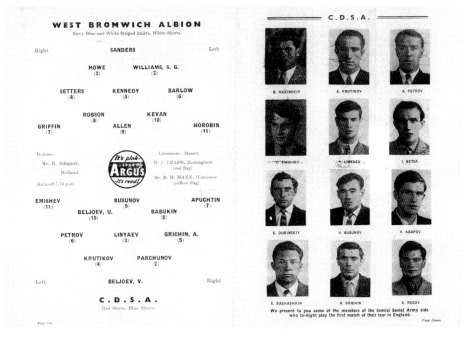

In 1957 West Bromwich Albion toured the Soviet Union. They were unbeaten in three games, two of which were won, including a 4-2 victory over the CDSA (Russian Red Army). They had a re-match against the Army side in October 1957 to officially switch on The Hawthorns floodlights and in front of 52,805 spectators and the TV cameras, the Baggies won a thrilling contest 6-5, Derek Kevan scoring twice. Here is the team line-up page from the programme, issued for that latter game.

Pictured here, from left to right, are four Walsall stalwarts from the 1950s: winger Fred Morris, inside forward/wing half Don Dorman, goalkeeper Reg Davies and full-back Bill 'Chopper' Guttridge. Between them they amassed well over 600 senior appearances for the Saddlers.

Above left: Jimmy Dudley, a member of West Bromwich Albion's 1954 FA Cup winning side, spent fifteen years at The Hawthorns, during which time he appeared in 320 first-class matches and scored 11 goals, and represented Scotland 'B'. Later he was a star wing half for Walsall (1959-64), making a further 175 senior appearances and helping the Saddlers rise from the Fourth to the Second Division in successive seasons.

Above right: Winger Norman Deeley, who was just 5ft 4ins tall, served Wolves from 1948 to 1962. During that time he scored 73 goals in 237 games, gained two League Championship and FA Cup winning medals (netting twice in the 1960 final *v.* Blackburn). Capped twice by England he also assisted Leyton Orient, Worcester City, Bromsgrove and Darlaston and for a time looked after the guest lounge at Fellows Park.

Date: August 1959. Venue: Molineux. Occasion: Billy Wright's last outing in a Wolves shirt (in the public practice match, Colours *v*. Whites). Here the great man, later to return as a director, shakes hands with the player who was to replace him in the Wolves defence, George Showell. Showell himself made 218 appearances for the Wanderers up until 1965, when he joined Bristol City.

Birmingham City's goalkeeper Johnny Schofield gets the better of West Bromwich Albion's centre forward Ronnie Allen during the local derby at The Hawthorns in April 1960. The game ended in a 1-1 draw, Albion having walloped Blues 7-1 at St Andrew's twenty-four hours earlier. The other players in the picture are Davey Burnside (left) and Derek Kevan (Albion) and Trevor Smith and Johnny Watts (Blues).

Pictured here is Walsall's promotion-winning side of 1960/61, when they finished runners-up in the Third Division. From left to right, back row: R. Faulkner, J. Davies, J. Christie (goalkeeper), J. Sharples, K. Ball (goalkeeper), J. Dudley, T. Rawlings. Front row: A. Richards, A. McPherson, W. Guttridge, H. Haddington, K. Hodgkisson, C. Taylor. On ground: K. Hill, N. Rowe, C. Askey and T. Foster.

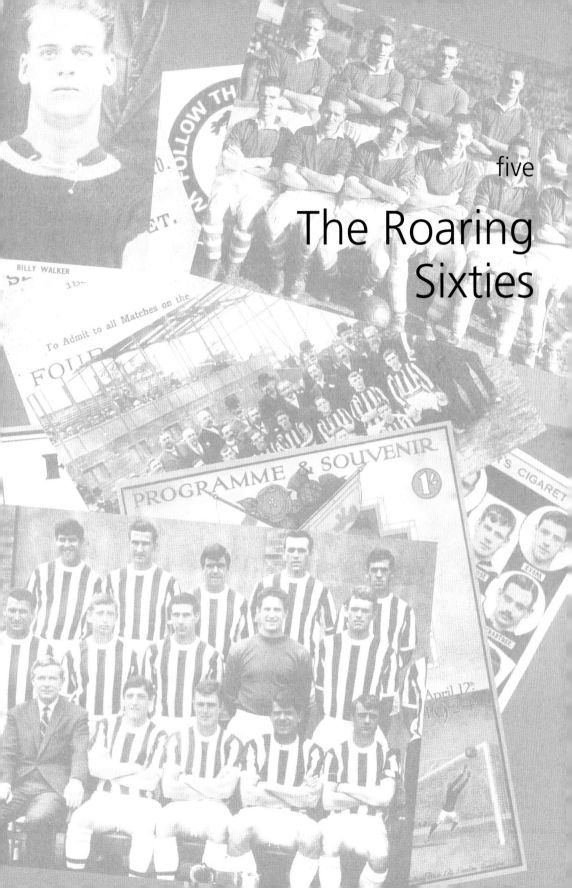

five

The Roaring
Sixties

In 1962/63 Walsall were relegated from the Second Division. After two wonderful campaigns (1959/60 and 1960/61), they had a moderate 1961/62 season, finishing fourteenth, before crashing through the relegation trapdoor and into the Third Division, where they were to stay until 1979. Here the players who were at Fellows Park in 1962/63. From left to right, back row: Tony Richards, John Sharples, Granville Palin, Alan Boswell, Jimmy Dudley, Trevor Foster, Gordon Wills. Seated: George Meek, Ken Hodgkisson, Albert McPherson (captain), Ken Hill, Colin Taylor.

Birmingham City, meanwhile, had a wonderful 1962/63 season. The Blues won the League Cup, beating arch-rivals Aston Villa 3-1 on aggregate in the final, after knocking out Doncaster Rovers, Barrow, Notts County, Manchester City and Bury. Here are most of the players who won that trophy, the first major pot (other than Second Division Championships) in the club's history. From left to right, back row: Graham Sissons, Trevor Smith, Johnny Schofield, Stan Lynn, Malcolm Beard, Terry Hennessey. Front row: Mike Hellawell, Bryan Orritt, Jimmy Harris, Len Leek, Bertie Auld.

In March 1963, a disappointing crowd of 18,217 witnessed a seven-goal thriller between Blues and Wolves at St Andrew's. The visitors won the contest 4-3 with goals from Ken Kirkham, Terry Wharton, Barry Stobart and Peter Broadbent, while Bertie Auld and two booming Stan Lynn penalties replied for the home side. Here, Blues striker Robin Stubbs (8) gets in a header. Team-mate Ken Leek (10) is behind him with the Wolves duo of Bobby Thomson (3) and Ron Flowers close at hand.

Seven months later, in October 1963, again at St Andrew's, a crowd of 24,804 saw Blues and Wolves draw 2-2 in a First Division match. In a cut-and-thrust contest, Alex Harley and Dave Woodfield (o.g.) scored for Blues while wingers Terry Wharton and Alan Hinton found the net for the visitors. The picture shows the Wolves 'keeper Fred Davies going the wrong way as the ball deflects into the net of his own defender (Woodfield).

IN ten years with glamorous, successful Wolves, play-ing in show games at home and abroad, regularly being capped for England, bland half-back dynamo RON FLOWERS has built up a wonderful soccer show-case.
Here he puts it on display, with the "medal shield" made by his uncle taking a prominent place.
Individual items are—
(1) CAPS — v. Luxembourg, Hungary, Mexico and Sweden. (2) CIGARETTE BOX — Wolves v. Celtic. (3) COFFEE SET—Yugoslavia v. England. (4-5) SPOONS and CLOCK — Italy v. England. (6) SKIS — Servette (Switzerland) v. Wolves. (7) DAGGER — Spain v. England. (8) ACQUAMARINE — Brazil v. England. (9) ASHTRAY — Peru v. England. (10) MODEL STADIUM — Barcelona v. Wolves. (11) BOTTLE OPENER—Denmark v. England. (12) SPOON—Durban v. Wolves. (13) ASHTRAY — Wolves v. Real Madrid. (14) WATCH — Real Madrid v. Wolves. (15) LIGHTER — Schalke (Germany) v. Wolves. (16) TIE PIN — England v. Italy. (17) SPRINGBOK — Nairobi v. Wolves. (18) FOOTBALL CLOCK — Anderlecht (Belgium) v. Wolves. (19-20-21) CHARITY SHIELDS — v. Notts F., Bolton and West Brom. (22) CLOCK — Stuttgart v. Wolves. (23) MEDAL — First Division Championship. (24) SHIELD — Northern Rhodesia v. Wolves. (25) F.A. CUP replica. (26) ASHTRAY — Valencia v. Wolves. (27-28) CHAMPIONSHIP CUP replicas. (29) BALL — Honved (Budapest) v. Wolves. (30) CAMERA — Russia v. England. (31) ASHTRAY — Wolves v. S. Africa. (32) STATUETTE — U.S.A. v. England. (33) SHIELD with medals — F.A. Cup, League, R.A.F., Wolves v. Gelsenkirchen, World Fair, etc.

Wing half Ron Flowers made 512 appearances for Wolves between 1952 and 1967, when he joined Northampton Town. A Football League Championship winner on three occasions (1954, 1958 and 1959) and FA Cup winner once (1960), he gained 49 caps for England and played in the World Cup finals.

Opposite, clockwise from top left:

Smethwick-born full-back Bobby Thomson made his senior debut for Wolves against WBA in the FA Cup in January 1962 – the first of 300 appearances for the club. He later played for Birmingham City (1969-72, playing in 69 games), Luton Town, Port Vale and Hartford Bi-Centennials (USA) and won 8 full caps for England.

Left-back Charlie Aitken made a record 660 appearances for Aston Villa, whom he served superbly from 1959 to 1976. A Third Division Championship and a League Cup winner in 1972 and 1975 respectively, he won 3 Scottish Under-23 caps and was voted 'Midland Footballer of the Year' in 1975.

Centre forward Gerry Hitchens joined Aston Villa from Cardiff in 1957 and left for Inter Milan in 1961. In those four years he hit 96 goals in 160 games, helping Villa win the Second Division title (1960) and reach the League Cup final (1961). He won 5 England caps, played for the Under-23s and the FA and also Torino, Cagliari and Atalanta in Italy.

Centre half Stan Jones made 265 appearances in two spells with Walsall (1957-60 and 1968-73) and 267 for Albion in between those times. Rock solid, he unfortunately missed three cup finals during his time at The Hawthorns (1966, 1967 and 1968) having already helped the Saddlers win the Fourth Division Championship in 1960.

Chelsea centre half John Mortimer climbs head and shoulders above West Bromwich Albion's Scottish-born left half Doug Fraser during the League game at Stamford Bridge in April 1965. Twenty-four hours before this match the Baggies had been crushed 6-1 by West Ham United at Upton Park, but they quickly bounced back to earn a point off Chelsea in a 2-2 draw, watched by almost 31,000 spectators. Gerry Howshall (with a beauty) and Ray Crawford scored for Albion. Fraser was signed from Aberdeen in 1963 and gained both League Cup and FA Cup winner's medals with Albion, while also playing in two losing League Cup finals (1967 and 1970). He made 325 appearances during his eight years at The Hawthorns before going on to serve Nottingham Forest and later Walsall, whom he also managed.

After winning the League Cup (1966) and losing in the final of the same competition a year later, Albion returned to Wembley in 1968 and won the FA Cup for the fifth time, beating Everton 1-0 after extra-time thanks to a Jeff Astle goal. En route to the Empire Stadium the Baggies, under the shrewd guidance of manager Alan Ashman, knocked out Colchester United and Southampton (both after replays), Portsmouth, Liverpool (after three games) and Birmingham City at Villa Park. Here is the victorious Albion team with Welsh international skipper Graham Williams in the forefront holding the trophy.

Right and below: Programme and ticket from that final.

Above left: Midfielder Danny Hegan had a varied career. Although born in Scotland, he played 7 times for Northern Ireland and in England served with Sunderland (two spells), Ipswich Town, West Bromwich Albion (1969-70) and Wolverhampton Wanderers (1970-73). He also played in South Africa and assisted Albion Rovers. He made 17 appearances for Albion and 70 for Wolves, helping the latter reach the 1972 UEFA Cup final.

Above right: Tall and efficient goalkeeper Phil Parkes was born in West Bromwich, but bypassed the Baggies to play for Wolves, for whom he made 382 appearances during his time at Molineux (1962-78). A Texaco Cup winner (1971) and UEFA Cup finalist (1972), he also played in the NASL with Vancouver Whitecaps, Toronto Blizzard, Chicago Sting and San Jose Earthquakes. Only Bert Williams and Mike Stowell have kept goal in more matches than 'Lofty' Parkes.

Opposite above: Ron Lewin managed Walsall during the first half of the 1968/69 season after taking over from the former WBA trainer Dick Graham. He was replaced in February 1969 when Bill Moore returned for a second spell in the hotseat at Fellows Park. The Saddlers huffed and puffed throughout this campaign before finishing thirteenth in the Third Division, having dropped six places from the previous year. This was the squad inherited by Lewin in the summer of 1968. From left to right, back row: Alan Baker, John Harris, Stan Jones, Alf Biggs, Trevor Meath, Jim Murray, John Burckitt. Middle row: Ray Cross, Mickey Evans, Bob Wesson, Phil Parkes, Keith Ball, Stan Bennett, Jimmy MacEwan (trainer). Front row: Geoff Morris, Nick Atthey, Tommy Watson, Lewin, Mike Tindall, Colin Harrison, Frank Gregg.

Above left: Jim Cumbes, besides being a very capable goalkeeper with (among others) Tranmere Rovers, West Bromwich Albion (1969-71) and Aston Villa (1971-76), was also a fast bowler who played county cricket for Warwickshire, Worcestershire, Lancashire and Surrey as well as West Bromwich Dartmouth. During his football career he amassed over 400 senior appearances (79 for Albion and 183 for Villa), helping the latter win the Third Division title (1972) and League Cup (1975). He is now chief executive of Lancashire CCC (Old Trafford).

Above right: Trevor Hockey was a football journeyman whose career spanned twenty years (1958-78) during which time he served with ten different clubs. He was a Birmingham City player from 1965-71, making 232 appearances, and spent the 1973/74 season at Villa Park (24 outings). He was capped 9 times by Wales and in all performed in more than 600 competitive games. He was only forty-three when he sadly died at a five-a-side tournament in his native Keighley in 1987.

In 1969/70 Walsall were managed by Bill Moore, the former Stoke City and Mansfield Town pre-war player, who was in his second spell in the Fellows Park hotseat. He had earlier been in office from 1957-63 and took over from Ron Lewin when he returned halfway through the 1968/69 season. The Saddlers had been having a tough time of things and did nothing outstanding in 1969/70, finishing twelfth in the Third Division, a rise of one place from the previous year. From left to right, back row: Colin Harrison, Trevor Meath, Stan Jones, Mick Evans, Derek Trevis. Second row: Jimmy MacEwan (trainer), Stan Bennett, Roy Cross, Bob Wesson, Phil Parkes, John Woodward, Frank Gregg, John Harris (reserve team trainer). Third row: Tommy Watson, Geoff Morris, Nick Atthey, Bill Moore, Alan Baker, Kenny Stephens, Dave Wilson. Front row: Terry Mighalls, Steve Williams, Chris Ainge, Gary Fleet, Keith Gough, Ray Train. Players Trevis, Woodward and Baker and also coaches Moore and MacEwan had all been associated with Aston Villa.

Above left: Albion's centre half John Talbut is beaten in the air during his side's 4-0 home European Cup-Winners' Cup victory over the Romanian side Dinamo Bucharest in November 1968. Talbut, signed from Burnley, made almost 200 appearances for Albion before losing his place to John Wile in 1971.

Above right: Arsenal goalkeeper Geoff Barnett is challenged by Baggies' striker Jeff Astle during the League game at Highbury in October 1969 which ended level at 1-1.

Opposite below: Like Walsall, West Midlands rivals Wolves also claimed thirteenth place in their Division (in this case the First). Under manager Bill McGarry, the Molineux side never got going and although they improved slightly by three places on their previous season's performance, they were going nowhere once the second half of the season got underway. In fact, they failed to win any of their last thirteen League games, losing eight of them (including four in a row right at the death when they failed to score a single goal). The Wanderers of 1969/70, from left to right, back row: Bernard Shaw, Gerry Taylor, John McAlle, Derek Dougan, Phil Parkes, Dave Woodfield, John Holsgrove, Frank Munro, Peter Knowles. Front row: Derek Clarke, John Farrington, Les Wilson, Mike Bailey (captain), Derek Parkin, Dave Wagstaffe, Paul Walker, Hugh Curran.

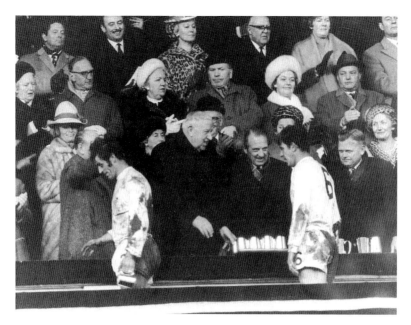

Albion reached the League Cup final three times in five years. In 1966 they defeated West Ham United over two legs, in 1967 they lost 3-2 to Queen's Park Rangers after leading 2-0, and then in 1970 they again went in front but in the end were beaten 2-1 by Manchester City after extra-time. Here, a dejected Baggies' skipper Doug Fraser, followed by John Kaye, make their way along the front of the Royal Box after collecting their loser's medals.

Above left: On 23 October 1971, Walsall celebrated the seventy-fifth anniversary of their election to the Football League and to commemorate the occasion this special First Day cover was issued.

Above right: In March 1972, Albion paid the unusual fee of £61,111 to Leicester City for Scottish-born striker Ally Brown. He did well at The Hawthorns, scoring 85 goals in 359 games for the Baggies before transferring to Crystal Palace in 1983. He later played for Walsall (1983-84) and Port Vale and also assisted Portland Timbers (NASL). He was later steward of The Hawthorns Throstle Club (Halfords Lane).

six

Into the
Seventies

Aston Villa and Walsall were locked together in the Third Division in 1970/71. The following season Villa gained promotion, while the Saddlers remained where they were until 1979 when they slipped down into the Fourth Division. In that 1970/71 campaign, Walsall matched Villa kick for kick during the two League games between the clubs and in fact came out on top, winning 3-0 at Fellows Park and then drawing 0-0 in the return fixture. The pictures here show action from the clash at Walsall. *Above:* Ex-Villa forward John Woodward (8) looks on as the referee blows up for foul on Villa 'keeper John Dunn. *Below:* Geoff Morris is congratulated after scoring one of his two goals. Colin Taylor rifled in a penalty for Walsall's third in front of more than 19,000 spectators – the biggest League crowd at Fellows Park for ten years.

Left: Jeff Astle completed ten years' dedicated service with West Bromwich Albion in 1974. A bargain buy by manager Jimmy Hagan at just £25,000 from Notts County, he scored 174 goals in 361 games for the Baggies, including the extra-time winner in the 1968 FA Cup final and one in each of two League Cup finals (1966 and 1970). He was capped 5 times by England and played in the World Cup finals in Mexico. Known as 'The King' he was adored by the fans who will never forget his tragic death during 2002.

Below left: Programme from Jeff's testimonial match in 1974.

Below right: Scottish international midfielder Asa Hartford was Jeff Astle's companion at The Hawthorns from 1967 to 1974. A wonderfully balanced and skilful footballer, he scored 26 goals in 275 games for the club before going on a nomadic tour of the UK, playing for Manchester City, Everton, Nottingham Forest, Norwich City, Stockport, Oldham Athletic, Bolton Wanderers and Shrewsbury Town, as well as having a spell in the NASL. He made over 800 career appearances and won 50 caps for Scotland. He was all set to join Leeds in 1971 but the deal broke down because of Hartford's heart complaint.

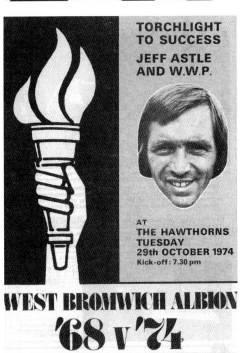

Wolves won the Football League Cup for the first time in 1974, beating Manchester City (winners over West Bromwich Albion four years earlier) 2-1 in a closely fought Wembley final. In their earlier rounds Bill McGarry's side knocked out Halifax Town, Tranmere Rovers (in a replay), Exeter City, Liverpool and Norwich City (over two legs in the semis). In the final a crowd of 97,886 saw Kenny Hibbitt open the scoring for Wolves; Colin Bell equalised and then up stepped ace marksman John Richards (pictured here) to score the winner.

During the 1970s there were three Latchford brothers all playing professional football at the same time. Goalkeeper Dave and centre forward Bob were registered with Birmingham City and another goalkeeper, Peter, was on the books of West Bromwich Albion. Between them they amassed a grand total of 537 senior appearances for the two Midland clubs, Dave and Bob clocking up 239 and 194 (plus 84 goals) respectively for Blues, and Peter 104 for the Baggies. Bob later played for Everton, Swansea City, Newport County, Blackpool, Coventry City, Lincoln City and NAC Breda of Holland, and won 12 caps for England, while Peter went on to assist Celtic (275 outings) and Clyde. Here Peter Latchford, the youngest of the trio (born in 1952), collects a high ball playing for Albion against West Ham United in 1973.

West Bromwich Albion played Second Division football from 1973 to 1976 before Johnny Giles got them back into the top flight. They were tough times at The Hawthorns until the former Manchester United, Leeds United and Republic of Ireland international arrived on the scene. He proceeded to do a wonderful job as the club's first-ever player-manager and when he left Albion were a pretty good side, good enough in fact to mount a challenge to play in Europe. Here you see Albion in action at Luton in a Second Division match in December 1975 – Baggies' goalkeeper John Osborne dives to push Steve Buckley's shot round the post in a 2-1 defeat.

After returning to the First Division, Albion produced some enterprising football, and conjured up some superb wins. Unfortunately they lost this encounter 1-0 to Manchester City at Maine Road in November 1976, despite some resolute defending by Ally Robertson (tackling Dennis Tueart) with full-back Paddy Mulligan (right).

WALSALL F.C. 1976-77

TOP (LEFT TO RIGHT): COLIN HARRISON, BERNIE WRIGHT, VINCE O'KEEFE, ROGER HYND, DAVE SERELLA, ROGER FRY.
MIDDLE (LEFT TO RIGHT): DOUG FRASER (TEAM MANAGER), BRIAN TAYLOR, ALAN BUCKLEY, DAVE ROBINSON, GEORGE ANDREWS, ALUN EVANS, MICK BATES.
BOTTOM (LEFT TO RIGHT): MIAH DENNEHY, KELVIN CLARKE, GARY SHELTON, IAN BRITTON, ALAN BIRCH.
INSETS: NICK ATTHEY (LEFT) AND BRIAN CASWELL (RIGHT).

The former West Bromwich Albion and Scottish international Doug Fraser was manager of Walsall in 1976/77, and after the team had finished eighth and seventh in Division Three the previous two seasons, he was quietly confident of doing better this time round. Alas, it was not to be as the Saddlers failed to produce the goods and ended up in fifteenth spot, nearer to the relegation zone than promotion.

At The Hawthorns Albion were improving all the time. They reached the FA Cup semi-finals in 1978 and, by finishing sixth in the First Division, duly qualified for the UEFA Cup, reaching the quarter-finals of that competition the following year when they rose to third place in the League table. At this point, Robson, Moses and manager Atkinson all left! Here you see one of Albion's stalwarts from the 1970s, John Wile, climbing above Southampton's Ted MacDougall during the 1-1 Tennent-Caledonian Cup draw at Ibrox Park, Glasgow, in August 1978 (Saints won the penalty shoot-out 3-1).

Above left: Bob Latchford scored 84 goals for Birmingham City whom he served as a professional for six years before transferring to Everton for a record fee of £350,000 (plus Howard Kendall) in 1974. A swashbuckling centre forward, he helped Blues gain promotion from the Second Division and formed a splendid striking-partnership with Trevor Francis and Bob Hatton. At Goodison Park he became a hero, netting 138 times in 289 outings for the Merseysiders (including 30 in 1977/78 when he became the first player to reach that target in top-flight football for six years, collecting a cheque for £10,000 for his efforts). Capped by England at Under-23 and senior levels, and honoured by the Football League, he went on to score almost 250 career goals (for clubs and country) in some 650 appearances.

Above centre: Mel Eves, born in Wednesbury, spent most of his career with Wolves whom he served for eleven years – 1973 to 1984. In that time he scored 53 goals in 214 first-class matches, gaining a League Cup winner's medal in 1980 when he played alongside Andy Gray. Later he assisted Sheffield United, West Bromwich Albion (reserves), Telford United and Cheltenham Town and was capped by England 'B' on 3 occasions. He's now a football agent, looking after the welfare of Albion's ex-Italian midfielder Enzo Maresca, among others.

Above right: Andy Gray, like Latchford, was an out-and-out goalscorer and during his career he too netted over 200 goals in more than 500 competitive games. Between 1972 and 1992, he played, in turn, for Dundee United, Aston Villa (1975-79), Wolves (1979-83), Everton, Villa again (1985-87), Notts County, West Bromwich Albion (1987-88), Glasgow Rangers and Cheltenham Town and was capped 20 times by Scotland while also representing his country at schoolboy, youth and Under-23 levels. He had the honour of scoring for the winning sides in the FA Cup, League Cup and European Cup-Winner's Cup finals, and gained League Championship medals with both Everton and Rangers. He was rewarded with both the 'Player's Player of the Year' and 'Young Player of the Year' trophies in 1977. Gray is now a prominent part of Sky Sports' Soccer team.

Above left: In 1977, West Bromwich Albion's brilliant winger Laurie Cunningham became the first black player to represent England at senior level when he starred in an Under-21 international against Scotland. Signed from Leyton Orient, he spent a little over two years at The Hawthorns, scoring 30 goals in 114 games before moving to Real Madrid for nearly £1 million. He later played for Manchester United, won an FA Cup winner's medal with Wimbledon and was capped 3 times by England. He also assisted several other foreign clubs prior to his tragic death in a car crash near Madrid in 1989.

Above centre: England youth international midfielder Ian 'Chico' Hamilton made his League debut as a teenager for Chelsea. He then had a spell with Sheffield United before netting 48 goals in 252 games for Aston Villa (1969-76). He returned to Bramall Lane and later assisted Minnesota Kicks (NASL). He played in two League Cup finals for Villa (who were winners in 1971 and losers in 1975) and helped them win the Third Division Championship in 1972.

Above right: Versatile, hard-tackling defender Garry Pendrey was one of Birmingham City's youngest-ever captains. He appeared in 357 games for Blues during his fourteen years at St Andrew's (1965-79), helping the team win promotion to the First Division in 1972. Thereafter he assisted West Bromwich Albion, Bristol Rovers and Walsall, managed Birmingham City (1987-89) and held coaching positions at Molineux, Coventry City and Southampton, the latter two under boss Gordon Strachan.

Right: Midfielder Bruce Rioch was the first English-born player to skipper Scotland. His career spanned almost twenty years (from 1964) and in that time he served with Luton, Aston Villa (1969-74), Derby County (two spells), Everton, Birmingham City (1977-79), Sheffield United, Seattle Sounders (NASL) and Torquay. He later managed at Plainmoor and also at Middlesbrough, Millwall, Norwich, Bolton, Arsenal and Wigan. He netted 37 goals in 176 games for Villa, won First and Third Division Championship medals with Derby and Villa respectively, gained promotion three times as a manager and won 24 full caps for his country.

Striker David Cross (left) and left-winger Willie Johnston were players together with West Bromwich Albion during the late 1970s. Cross, in fact, returned for a second spell in 1984 and scored a total of 23 goals in 62 games for the club. A soccer journeyman, he also assisted Rochdale, Norwich City, Coventry, West Ham, Manchester City, Vancouver Whitecaps, Oldham Athletic, Bolton, Bury and Blackpool. He was an FA Cup winner with the Hammers (1980). Johnston was Albion's record signing when joining from Glasgow Rangers in 1972, recruited after he had just served a 28-day suspension. He won League, SFA Cup, League Cup and ECWC medals whilst at Ibrox Park and eventually collected 22 full caps. He bagged 28 goals in 261 games for the Baggies (up to 1979) and afterwards had spells with Vancouver Whitecaps (twice), Birmingham City, Rangers (again), Hearts and South China before taking up coaching. A fiery character, he was sent off 17 times during his career. He is now a publican in Kirkcaldy.

Clockwise from top left:

Centre half Joe Gallagher made 335 appearances for Birmingham City between 1970 and 1981. He played next for Wolves for sixteen months after signing for £350,000, and later served with West Ham United, Burnley and Halifax Town.

Between them the Scottish duo of Ally Robertson and Doug Fraser appeared in over 950 games for West Bromwich Albion, the former amassing 626 to the latter's 325. 'Robbo' later played for Wolves (late 1980s), helping them win promotion and the Sherpa Van trophy at Wembley. Fraser, a League Cup and FA Cup winner with Albion, was a full international who also played for Aberdeen (his first club), Nottingham Forest and Walsall – who he also managed in the late 1970s.

Rock-solid, Jamaican-born central defender Noel Blake played for Walsall, Aston Villa (1979-82), Shrewsbury Town and Birmingham City (1982-84) as well as for Leeds United, Portsmouth, Stoke City, Bradford City, Dundee and Exeter City during a career covering more than twenty years. He was manager of the lattermost club in 2000/01.

Defender/midfielder Nick Atthey lies second behind Colin Harrison in the all-time list of Walsall appearance-makers. Between 1963 and 1977 he played in 502 first-class matches (439 in the League) and was a totally committed and dedicated footballer who later in life served with Rushall Olympic.

In December 1976 Aston Villa produced a wonderful display of attacking football to destroy the reigning League Champions and First Division leaders Liverpool 5-1 in front of 42,851 fans at Villa Park. Here is Villa's fourth goal, scored by Brian Little. John Deehan and Andy Gray shared the others between them on a night when the red half of Merseyside all had 'red' faces.

Local derbies – no matter where – always bring a touch of passion and commitment to the game, although perhaps none more so than clashes involving Villa and Blues and Albion and Wolves. Here we see six-yard box action involving goalkeeper Jim Montgomery and Garry Pendrey (Blues) and John Deehan (Villa) during the Second City derby at Villa Park in October 1977, when a crowd of 45,536 saw the visitors win 1-0.

At the end of the 1977/78 season West Bromwich Albion visited Hong Kong and The People's Republic of China – becoming the first professional club to play a competitive match in the latter country. The tour, arranged jointly by The Football Association and London Export Corporation, was a huge success. Albion played a total of five matches and won them all, defeating Peking XI 3-1, China 2-0, Shanghai 2-0, Kwantung Province 6-0 and Hong Kong Select 3-0. Each game was played in front of a capacity crowd with 88,400 present for the clash against the Chinese National team and 80,000 for the fixture in Peking. Above, Albion directors Brian Boundy, Cliff Edwards (an ex-player) and Sid Lucas (later club chairman) ponder whether to visit the Great Wall as they arrive in China.

BRITISH FOOTBALL
TOUR TO CHINA
MAY 1978

"Friendship first, competition second"

WEST BROMWICH ALBION

TOUR ARRANGED JOINTLY BY
THE FOOTBALL ASSOCIATION AND
LONDON EXPORT CORPORATION

OFFICIAL TOUR PROGRAMME

Left: Official tour programme.

In 1980 Wolves won the Football League Cup for the second time, beating Nottingham Forest 1-0 at Wembley thanks to a gift goal presented on a plate for Andy Gray. The top picture shows Wolves' goalkeeper Paul Bradshaw (later of WBA) plucking the ball away from Forest's Kenny Burns (formerly of Birmingham City) and below the joyous Wolves players celebrating victory – from left to right, striker Mel Eves, full-back Geoff Palmer, midfielder Kenny Hibbitt, goalkeeper Paul Bradshaw (behind his skipper), Scottish international Willie Carr, left-back Derek Parkin and bearded centre half and Welsh international George Berry. The Wolves manager was John Barnwell, a former Forest player.

Above left: John Burridge's career spanned four decades and lasted almost thirty years (1968-97). In that time he played in more than 1,000 matches (915 at competitive level) and served with twenty-three different clubs including Aston Villa (1975-78) and Wolves (1982-84). He was also registered with Blackpool, Crystal Palace, QPR, Sheffield United, Newcastle and Aberdeen, among others all over the UK. He even coached in China.

Above centre: Tony Godden made his name with West Bromwich Albion, whom he served from 1975 to 1986, making a total of 329 appearances of which 228 were consecutive (a club record). He also played for Gillingham (briefly), Wolves (as an amateur trialist), Chelsea, Birmingham City (1987-89), Preston North End, Luton Town, Walsall and Sheffield Wednesday. He is now a respected goalkeeping coach.

Above right: Jeff Wealands started his career at Molineux in 1968. He was not a success with Wolves, however, and moved to Northampton Town, later assisting Darlington, Hull City, Birmingham City (119 appearances during 1979-83), Manchester United (on loan), Oldham Athletic, Preston North End, Altrincham and Barrow. As non-League Altrincham's 'keeper, he returned to St Andrew's in 1985 and helped knock Blues out of the FA Cup.

Right: Mark Grew understudied Tony Godden at The Hawthorns for many years. He was an Albion player from 1976 to 1983 and again in 1986 and made a total of 48 appearances for the club. He also played for Wigan Athletic, Port Vale, Notts County, Leicester City, Oldham Athletic, Ipswich Town, Fulham and Derby County and was later employed as a coach at Vale Park. He made his senior debut in the UEFA Cup and played in both the League Cup and FA Cup semi-finals for Albion in 1982.

seven

The Exciting Eighties

In 1981 Aston Villa became the first Midland club to win the Football League Championship for twenty-two years (since Wolves' success in 1959) and a year later they carried off the coveted European Cup, beating Bayern Munich 1-0 in the final in Rotterdam, Peter Withe knocking in the all-important goal. *Above left:* Midfielder Dennis Mortimer, Villa's skipper at the time, made over 400 appearances for the club, whom he served for ten years (1975-85). He also played for Coventry City, Sheffield United and Birmingham City and was later associated with West Bromwich Albion.

Above right: Thousands of supporters flocked to the centre of Birmingham to congratulate Ron Saunders' men on their League success and the same applied when Tony Barton guided the team to European glory in Holland.

Tony Morley, a key member of Villa's side, was a dashing left-winger who had a wonderful career with Preston North End, Burnley, Aston Villa (1979-83), West Bromwich Albion (1983-84 and 1987-88) and Birmingham City (1984), as well as playing in America, Japan, Holland, Malta and New Zealand. He scored over 65 goals in more than 450 competitive games and gained 6 full caps for England.

Tony Brown was, to many supporters, 'Mr West Bromwich Albion'. He served the club for twenty years (1961-81) and in that time broke and set records galore. He scored 279 goals in 720 first-class matches, 218 coming in 574 League games. He gained winner's prizes for both the League Cup (1966) and FA Cup (1968), helped Albion regain their First Division status (1976), was capped by England (*v.* Wales in 1971) and also represented the Football League and his country's youth team. A wholehearted attacking midfielder, born in Oldham in 1945, he was voted 'Midland Footballer of the Year' in 1969, 1971 and 1979. After retiring he coached at The Hawthorns and Birmingham City.

Derek Statham played in the same Albion team as 'Bomber' Brown. The attacking left-back served the club from 1975 to 1987, during which time he appeared in 378 senior games and scored 10 goals. He was capped 3 times by England and would have certainly gained a lot more honours had Kenny Sansom not been around at the same time. He also represented his country at 'B', Under-21 and youth team levels, and in 1978 was voted the Midlands 'Young Player of the Year'. After leaving The Hawthorns Statham played for Southampton, Stoke City and Walsall and now runs a café-bar in Spain.

Many clubs – including Aston Villa, West Bromwich Albion and Wolves – have a former players' association and they fulfil several charity matches each season, travelling within a fifty-mile radius of the area. Between 1979 and 1989, the Albion All Stars played over 150 games and lost only 3, raising thousands of pounds for good causes and even going on tour to the Caribbean. Here, an Albion 'old stars' XI face the camera before a game against Campden Town in 1981. From left to right, back row: Campbell Crawford, Alec Jackson, Stan Jones, Geoff Barnsley, Graham Lovett, Bob Green, Geoff Snape. Front row: Ron Jukes, Mick Robertson, Tony Matthews, Bobby Hope, Graham Smith. Jackson, Hope and Smith also played for Birmingham City and Jones was centre half for Walsall.

Above left: David Kelly, like Bertschin, had an excellent career as a goalscorer. Born in Birmingham in 1965, he was an Albion fan as a lad and started out with Alvechurch before joining Walsall, for whom he netted 80 goals in 190 games. He then served with West Ham, Leicester City, Newcastle United, Wolves (1993-95 – playing alongside Steve Bull and notching 36 goals in 103 outings), Sunderland, Tranmere Rovers, Sheffield United and Motherwell. He was capped 26 times by the Republic of Ireland and played in 'B' and Under-21 internationals. He ended up with over 240 goals in 725 club games.

Above right: Striker Keith Bertschin started his career with Barnet and, after a spell with Ipswich Town, joined Birmingham City in 1977. He scored 41 goals in 141 games for Blues and then went on to play for Norwich City, Jacksonville Teamen (NASL), Stoke City, Sunderland, Walsall (1988-90), Chester City and Aldershot before dropping into non-League football. Capped 3 times by England Under-21s, he netted over 150 goals during his fifteen-year career.

As mentioned earlier, Second City derbies can be either exciting, tedious, boring or a waste of time... There have now been 98 'League' derbies between Aston Villa and Birmingham City and it is Villa who have the better overall record (at 2004) with 39 wins against the 32 of Blues. Very few of these encounters have taken place outside the top-flight and in a rare Second Division contest, played in August 1987, Blues won 2-0 at Villa Park in front of almost 31,000 spectators, Ian Handysides and Tony Rees the scorers. Here, Blues' full-back Brian Roberts (who also played for Coventry City and Wolves) gets in a tackle on Villa and England's Mark Walters.

Staffordshire derbies involving West Bromwich Albion and Stoke City began in the 1880s and, in fact, the clubs met each other on the opening day of the Football League competition – 8 September 1888 when Albion won 2-0 in the Potteries. Now there have been 116 such League games involving two of the founder members and at the minute (at 2004) it is Stoke who have the better set of statistics with 49 wins to their credit against Albion's 38. A floodlit First Division match at the Victoria Ground in September 1982 ended in a 3-0 win for Albion in front of a crowd of 17,446. Here Mark Chamberlain, the Potters' winger, despite a challenge from Albion defender Ally Robertson, gets in a shot at 'keeper Mark Grew with Martyn Bennett (5) and Clive Whitehead close at hand.

Above left: Tipton-born striker Steve Bull was given away by Albion in 1986 and went on to score over 300 goals for Wolves, setting records by the seasons and helping the Molineux club rise from the Fourth to the Third Division and win the Sherpa Van Trophy at Wembley. He also gained 13 caps for England and was awarded the MBE in 1994.

Above centre: Left-back Tony Dorigo was born in Australia, played for Aston Villa (1981-87, making 135 appearances), Chelsea, Leeds United, Torino (Italy), Derby County and Stoke City. He won 15 caps for England, played for the Under-21 and 'B' teams and helped Leeds win the First Division title. He retired with over 650 senior appearances under his belt.

Above right: Striker Kevin Summerfield started his career with Albion with whom he gained a Youth Cup winner's medal in 1976 (*v.* Wolves). He then assisted Blues (1982), Walsall (1982-84), Cardiff, Plymouth, Exeter and Shrewsbury, netting 81 goals in 460 senior games. He returned to Home Park as a coach and later was made caretaker-manager before joining Southampton as part of Paul Sturrock's short-lived managerial regime in 2004. He is now assistant manager at Sheffield Wednesday.

Left: In a twenty-year career Birmingham-born England Under-21 striker Garry Thompson hit 153 goals in 573 senior games while playing for Coventry, Albion (1983-85 – 45 goals in 105 outings), Sheffield Wednesday, Aston Villa (1986-88 – 19 goals in 73 games), Watford, Crystal Palace, QPR, Cardiff City and Northampton. Later he managed Bristol Rovers.

Above left: Ex-Manchester United and Leeds midfielder Johnny Giles became West Bromwich Albion's first-ever player-manager in 1975. Two years later he guided the Baggies to promotion from the Second Divison. Capped 50 times by the Republic of Ireland, he played in eleven FA Cup semi-finals and five FA Cup finals and scored 125 goals in 863 career appearances (1959-77). Also player-boss of Shamrock Rovers, coach of Vancouver Whitecaps and manager of his country, he had a disappointing second spell in charge at The Hawthorns in the mid-1980s.

Above centre: Versatile defender Phil Hawker served with Birmingham City (1978-82), Walsall (to 1990), West Bromwich Albion (on loan) and Kidderminster Harriers. An England youth international, he made 37 appearances for Blues, 221 for Walsall but only one for Albion.

Above right: Centre half Ken McNaught was in Aston Villa's League Championship and European Cup winning sides of 1981 and 1982. He started out with Everton, joined Villa for £200,000 in 1977 and after 260 games was transferred to West Bromwich Albion for £125,000 in 1983. He played in exactly 50 games for the Baggies and after a loan spell with Manchester City he left The Hawthorns for Sheffield United and was later associated with Dunfermline Athletic and Swansea. His father, Willie, was a Scottish international. Ken himself now works in the pro's shop at the Gleneagles golf course.

Right: Steve Hunt played for Coventry City, Aston Villa, West Bromwich Albion, New York Cosmos and England during his fourteen-year career (1973-1987).

Above left: Ian Handysides sadly died of cancer at the age of twenty-seven, having played for Birmingham City, Walsall, Wolves and England youth. An eager-beaver midfielder he scored 12 goals in 133 games for Blues in two spells at St Andrew's (1978-84 and 1986), struck 11 in 81 for the Saddlers and as a loanee scored twice in 11 outings for Wolves.

Above centre: Dean Peer, from Wordsley, Stourbridge, was a midfield player who made 150 appearances for Birmingham City during his eight years at St Andrew's (1985-93). He also assisted Mansfield Town, Walsall (1993-95), Northampton Town and Shrewsbury, finishing up with Moor Green in 2001. He scored a hat-trick for the 'Shrews' shortly after his move to Gay Meadow.

Above right: Tony Grealish was a gritty, no-nonsense midfielder whose career lasted twenty years (1972-92). He began with Leyton Orient, switched to Luton in 1979 and four years later played for Brighton in the FA Cup final. He moved to West Bromwich Albion in 1984, played next for Manchester City (after 5 goals in 76 games for the Baggies) and following spells with Rotherham and FC Salgueros (Portugal) he became player-coach of Walsall, later assisting ex-Albion stars Bobby Hope at Bromsgrove and Steve Mackenzie at Atherstone. Grealish was capped 47 times by the Republic of Ireland.

Right: Colin Anderson, like Grealish, also played in midfield and also at full-back for Albion and Walsall. He started his professional career with Burnley in 1980 and after spells with North Shields, Torquay United and QPR he moved to The Hawthorns in 1985. He appeared in 152 games for the Baggies (12 goals scored) and then went on to play for Walsall (for whom he made 29 appearances in 1991/92), Hereford United and finally Exeter City (until 1996).

Clockwise from top:

In 1988/89 Wolves, under manager Graham Turner and with Steve Bull again banging in the goals, raced away with the Third Division Championship, amassing 92 points from 26 wins and 14 draws. They suffered only 6 defeats, one of them at Northampton Town who cobbled the Wanderers 3-1 in front of almost 6,500 fans at the County Ground. Here Wolves left-back Andy Thompson, who was signed with Bull from neighbouring West Bromwich Albion, gets in a challenge on Town's Dean Thomas. Later in the campaign Wolves won the return fixture at Molineux 3-2.

Midfielder Paul 'Pee-Wee' Dougherty stood only 5ft 2ins tall, making him one of the smallest players ever to serve Wolves at senior level. He scored 5 goals in 47 appearances between 1984 and 1987 and later assisted Torquay United and San Diego and had a trial with West Bromwich Albion.

Between 1973 and 1991 left-back Brian 'Harry' Roberts made a total of 428 League appearances while serving with four different clubs: Coventry City, Hereford United, Birmingham City and Wolves, having by far his best days at Highfield Road. He later became a coach and wrote a book: *Harry's Game*.

Above left: Fast-raiding winger Tony Daley scored 38 goals in 290 games for Aston Villa and gained 7 England caps before Wolves paid a record fee of £1.25 million for his services in June 1994. He struggled with injuries at Molineux and after being released played for Watford and Forest Green Rovers, helping the non-League club reach the final of the FA Trophy at his former home, Villa Park, in 2001.

Above centre: After only a handful of first-team games winger Robbie Dennison left West Bromwich Albion for Wolves in a £40,000 deal in 1986. He did superbly well at Molineux, scoring 49 goals in 353 outings and won 18 caps for Northern Ireland while also playing at Wembley, helping Wolves win the Sherpa Van Trophy and twice gain promotion. Later he assisted Swansea Town, Hednesford and Hereford United.

Above right: The versatile Chris Marsh appeared in 426 League and cup games for Walsall between 1987 and 1989. Able to occupy a defensive or midfield role, he currently lies tenth in the list of Saddlers' all-time appearance-makers.

Left: Gary Childs was at Fellows Park just before Marsh. A midfielder, he started his career with West Bromwich Albion, played next for Walsall (1983-87) and then served with Birmingham City and Grimsby Town, making 520 League appearances in all.

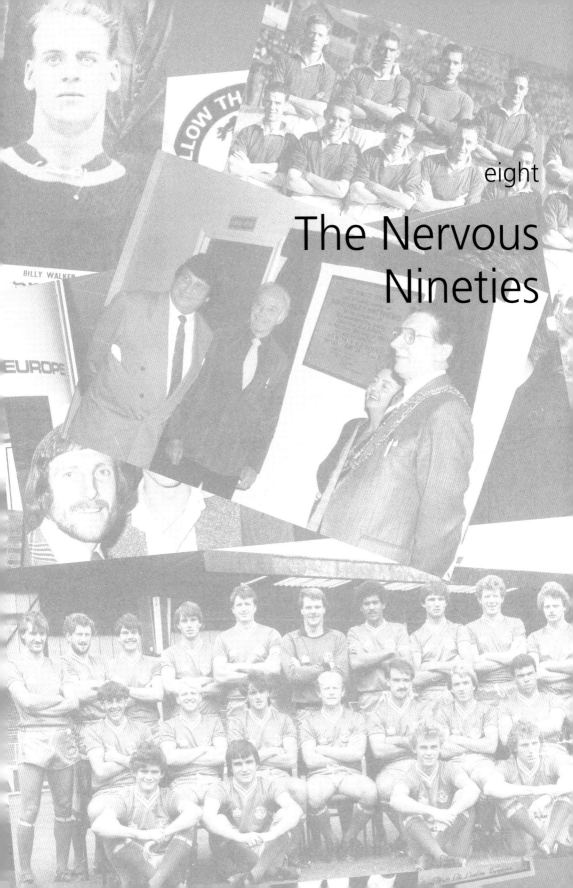

eight

The Nervous
Nineties

These four players were all associated with Birmingham City and West Bromwich Albion.

Above left: Winger Dave Smith also assisted Coventry City, Bournemouth and Grimsby Town and gained 10 England Under-21 caps.

Above centre: Welsh international centre half Paul Mardon started his career with Bristol City and besides his time at St Andrew's and The Hawthorns, he also played for Doncaster Rovers, Oldham Athletic, Plymouth Argyle and Wrexham. He was forced to retire in 2001 through injury.

Above right: Defender Chris Whyte made his League debut for Arsenal in the late 1970s. He then assisted Crystal Palace and played in the NASL before returning to England with Albion. After serving with Leeds United and Blues, he rounded off an interesting career with Coventry City, Charlton Athletic, West Ham, Leyton Orient, Oxford United and Rushden & Diamonds, while also having another stint in the USA with Detroit.

Left: The career of Scottish international forward David Speedie spanned eighteen years (1977-95). During that time he was associated with eleven different clubs, including Barnsley (his first), Blackburn Rovers, Chelsea, Leicester City, Liverpool and Southampton as well as Blues and Albion. He won 10 full caps and scored 175 goals in 611 senior games.

'Super' Bob Taylor – an Albion Great – scored 131 goals in two spells with the Baggies (1992-98 and 2000-03). This is his 100th – headed home against Derby County at the Hawthorns. Still in the game today with Tamworth, he started out with Leeds United, played next for Bristol City and in between his spells at The Hawthorns, appeared and scored for Bolton Wanderers in the Premiership.

Above left: Prior to Taylor, Cyrille Regis was another huge favourite with the Albion fans. He netted 112 goals in 302 outings during his seven years with the club (1977-84) and after leaving he collected an FA Cup winner's medal with Coventry City (1987) before going on to assist Aston Villa, Wolves, Wycombe Wanderers and Chester City. The recipient of 5 England caps, he returned to The Hawthorns as a reserve team coach and is now a football agent.

Above right: Canadian-born striker Paul Peschisolido has scored goals wherever he's played – doing so for Toronto Blizzard, Kansas City Comets, Birmingham City (1992-94), Stoke City, West Bromwich Albion (1996-97), Fulham, Queen's Park Rangers, Sheffield United, Norwich City and Derby County. He has played in 50 full and 11 Under-23 internationals and also starred in 9 matches in the Olympic Games.

Birmingham City went through a difficult period during the mid-to-late-1980s when their form on the pitch was poor. Attendances at home games slumped to a seasonal average of 6,289 and players were coming and going at an alarming rate. At the end of 1988/89, with ex-defender Garry Pendrey having been in charge, Blues were relegated to the Third Division for the first time in the club's history. These were bad times at St Andrew's. As a result Pendrey was replaced by the former Spurs and Scotland international Dave Mackay who had been manager of Derby County. Although occasionally the team did produce a spirited performance on the field, they had to settle for seventh place in the Third Division the following year and in fact, didn't climb out of this section until 1992 (under the guidance of Terry Cooper). In April 1990 Bristol Rovers visited St Andrew's and in front of 12,438 supporters – the biggest League gate at the ground since December 1987 – Blues were held to a 2-2 draw, having been two-up after 19 minutes through Robert Hopkins and Trevor Matthewson. The top picture shows Rovers striker Devon White heading home on 58 minutes to reduce the deficit, and the bottom one shows Carl Saunders on hand to grab the equaliser. This summed up Blues' fortunes at this time – they let too many games slip away having been in control and looking likely winners.

Much-travelled striker Andy Saville served with Hull City, Walsall, Barnsley and Hartlepool before joining Birmingham City for £155,000 in March 1993. He went on to score 18 goals in 65 appearances up to July 1995 when he transferred to Preston North End, having been on loan to Burnley prior to that. He later assisted Wigan Athletic, Cardiff City, Hull (again) and Scarborough before pulling out of competitive football in 1999 with more than 135 goals to his credit in 515 games.

Midfielders Nigel Gleghorn (in the striped shirt of Stoke City) and Paul Birch (Wolves) both started their League careers in the mid-1980s – Gleghorn with Ipswich Town and Birch with Aston Villa. Gleghorn went on to play for Manchester City, Birmingham City (1989-92 – playing in 176 games and claiming 43 goals), Stoke, Burnley, Brentford and Northampton Town, ending up with a career record of 461 League appearances and 83 goals. Birch was born in West Bromwich and scored 25 goals in 219 outings for his first club, Aston Villa. He then served, in turn, with Wolves (1991-96 – making 166 appearances and netting 19 goals), Preston North End, Doncaster Rovers and finally Exeter City. His elder brother, Alan, also played for Wolves as well as Walsall, Chesterfield, Barnsley, Scunthorpe United and Stockport County. Between them the Birches accumulated a total of 884 League appearances.

Stoke City and Wolves – both founder members of the Football League in 1888 – have now played each other more than 150 times at various levels. Wolves have by far the better overall record in terms of wins – and one of their best came in a replayed FA Cup tie back in 1889. Initially Wolves won the first contest 4-0, but the Potters complained about the state of the pitch. A replay was ordered and this time Wolves won 8-0 with Jack Brodie scoring five times. The picture here shows goalmouth action from the League game at Molineux in October 1995 featuring Don Goodman and Neil Emblem (Wolves) and Ray Wallace, Lee Sandford and Nigel Gleghorn (Stoke). A crowd of 26,483 saw the Potters win 4-1 with goals from Gleghorn, Graham Potter (who also played for Albion and Birmingham City), Ray Wallace and Martin Carruthers (ex-Aston Villa). Former Albion man Andy Thompson (penalty) replied for Wolves.

Right: Left-back Paul Agnew (in the stripes of Grimsby Town) and utility forward Louie Donowa (Birmingham City) clash in a League game at St Andrew's. Agnew, a Northern Ireland schoolboy, youth and Under-21 international, made over 250 appearances for the Mariners (1984-95) before joining his former manager Alan Buckley at West Bromwich Albion. He later assisted Swansea City. Donowa's career spanned sixteen years (1982-98) and in that time he served with twelve different clubs including two spells at Walsall (1996/97 and 1997/98). Capped by England at Under-21 level, he also played for Norwich City, Stoke City, Burnley and, of course, Blues (1991-96) for whom he made 168 appearances and scored 19 goals.

In August 1998, West Bromwich Albion recruited two Italian midfield players – Mario Bortolazzi (left) and Enzo Maresca – the first footballers from that country ever to represent the Baggies. The thirty-three-year-old Bortolazzi, vastly experienced, had already played in more than 300 games in his homeland while serving with AC Milan, Atalanta, Fiorentina, Genoa, Parma and Verona. He appeared in 36 games in English football before joining Lecce. The highly talented Maresca (right) was just eighteen at the time and he remained at The Hawthorns until January 2000 when he switched to Juventus for £4.5 million. An Italian youth, Under-20 and Under-21 international he later played for Bologna and Piacenza. He scored 5 goals in 53 outings for the Baggies. Former Wolves striker Mel Elves is now Maresca's agent.

Left: Centre half Paul McGrath, seen here in a First Division clash with Oldham Athletic striker Sean McCarthy, made 203 appearances for Manchester United before joining Aston Villa in 1989 for what was to prove a bargain fee of £450,000. He added a further 323 appearances to his tally during his time at Villa Park, collecting two League Cup winners' medals in 1994 and 1996. He later served with Derby County and Sheffield United and was capped 83 times by the Republic of Ireland.

Above left: Steve Staunton, seen here leading out Aston Villa with his Grimsby Town counterpart, Paul Futcher, for an FA Cup tie in 1998, holds the record for most caps for the Republic of Ireland: 103. He started out with Dundalk, played next for Liverpool (from 1986), had a loan spell with Bradford City, signed for Villa in 1991 (for £1.1m), returned to Anfield, and after a loan spell with Crystal Palace, he came back to Villa Park and is now with Coventry City. A League Championship, FA Cup and League Cup winner, he has now amassed around 650 appearances at club and international level.

Above right: The versatile Neil Emblen had two spells with Wolves (1994–97 and 1998-2001) and he has also played for Millwall, Crystal Palace, Norwich City and Walsall, joining the latter in 2003. He reached the milestone of 300 club appearances in 2004, having made 234 during his association with Wolves.

Above left: Midfielder Martin O'Connor, who was born in Walsall in 1967, started his League career with Crystal Palace before moving to his home-town club in 1994 (after a loan spell at the Bescot Stadium). He switched to Peterborough United in 1996, transferred to Birmingham City for £500,000 later that same year and returned to the Saddlers for a second spell in 2002. A Cayman Island international, he made almost 180 appearances for Walsall and 223 for the Blues.

Above centre: London-born goalkeeper Alan Miller played for Arsenal, Plymouth Argyle, West Bromwich Albion (two spells: 1991 and 1997-2000, making a total of 110 appearances), Birmingham City (on loan in 1991, 16 outings), Middlesbrough, Grimsby Town, Blackburn Rovers, Bristol City, Coventry City and St Johnstone. A fine shot-stopper, he gained 4 England Under-21 caps, was a European Cup-winner's Cup winner with the Gunners (1994) and helped Middlesbrough win the Division One title (1995).

Above right: Welsh international Dean Saunders was a prolific marksman who scored 276 goals in 806 appearances for clubs and country. Like Barber (below), he moved around quite a bit, playing for Swansea City, Cardiff City, Brighton, Oxford United, Derby County, Liverpool, Aston Villa (1992-95, netting 49 goals in 144 outings), Galatasaray (Turkey), Nottingham Forest, Sheffield United, Benfica (Portugal) and Bradford City. Capped 75 times, he was an FA Cup winner (1992) with Liverpool and a League Cup winner with Villa (1994). He is now a coach at Newcastle.

Right: Over a period of seventeen years from 1979, Fred Barber became a goalkeeping journeyman who played for twelve different League clubs including Walsall (189 appearances), Luton Town, Ipswich Town, Blackpool, Peterborough United (three spells), Birmingham City (one outing in January 1996) and Everton. He later became a goalkeeper coach, with West Bromwich Albion among his employers. A bit of a joker, he once took the field wearing a horror mask.

In the summer of 1996, Blues manager Trevor Francis spent almost £3 million on five players, acquired in double-quick time. He bought defender Gary Ablett (top left), striker Paul Furlong (centre), centre half Steve Bruce (top right), midfielder Barry Horne (above, left) and frontman Mike Newell. Ablett had made over 300 appearances while serving with Merseyside clubs, Everton and Liverpool. He also played for Derby County, Hull City, Sheffield United, Wycombe Wanderers, Scunthorpe United and Blackpool. He had 124 outings with Blues. Furlong, the dearest of the quintet at £1.5m, repaid a fair bit of that money by scoring 56 goals in 153 games for Blues before moving to QPR. He had previously played for Coventry City, Watford and Chelsea and gained 5 caps for England semi-professionals with Enfield (1989-91). Bruce had played in 425 games for Manchester United during his nine years at Old Trafford. He had started out with Gillingham, played next for Norwich and later became Blues' manager following similar appointments at Sheffield United, Huddersfield and Crystal Palace. His successes included three Premiership wins, two FA Cup final triumphs, the League Cup, European Cup-winners Cup and Super Cup and in 2002 he took Blues into the Premiership, having made 82 appearances during his time as a player at St Andrew's. Horne had already assisted Wrexham, Portsmouth, Southampton and Everton before moving to St Andrew's. He made only 40 appearances for Blues who transferred him to Huddersfield in 1997. A Welsh international, capped 59 times, he later played for Sheffield Wednesday, Kidderminster Harriers and Walsall.

Newell, who is now manager at his old hunting ground, Kenilworth Road, was a goalscorer with Crewe Alexandra, Wigan Athletic, Luton Town, Leicester City, Everton and Blackburn Rovers before joining Blues. He failed to hit the heights at St Andrew's (3 strikes in 20 outings) and left for Aberdeen after loan spells with West Ham and Bradford City. He returned to Gresty Road in 1999 and then assisted Doncaster Rovers and Blackpool before taking over as manager of Hartlepool (2002), moving to Luton in the same capacity a year later. Honoured by England at 'B' and Under-21 levels, Newell helped Blackburn win the Premiership title in 1995 when he teamed up with Alan Shearer.

nine

Forward Into a New Century

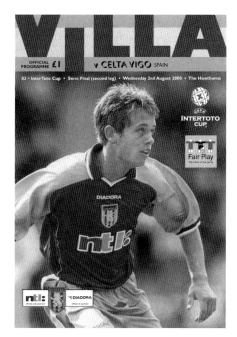

UEFA INTERTOTO CUP

Aston Villa -v- F.C. Marila Pribram

Smethwick End

Kick-Off 2:00 PM

Admit Turnstiles: B1 - B5

This ticket is Non-Refundable   10.00

Your account No:

TO BE RETAINED UNTIL END OF MATCH

Left and above: In the build-up to the 2000/01 season Aston Villa participated in the InterToto Cup and had to play two home games at The Hawthorns. One was against Celta Vigo who recorded a 2-1 win (Bennie McCarthy netting both goals), having also triumphed 1-0 in the first leg in Spain. Three players were sent off in the second leg – Villa's Ian Taylor and Alan Thompson and Vigo's Velasso.

Above left: Derek McInness skippered West Bromwich Albion when they gained promotion to the Premiership in 2002. The Scottish-born midfielder, previously with Morton, Glasgow Rangers, Toulouse (France) and Stockport County, made exactly 100 appearances for the Baggies and represented his country at senior level before joining Dundee United.

Above right: Striker Uwe Rosler also helped Albion climb out of the First Division in 2002. Capped 5 times by East Germany before unification, he was the first footballer from that country ever to play for the Baggies, scoring once in five starts when on loan from Southampton. He had earlier played for FC Nuremburg, Manchester City, FC Kaiserslautern and Tennis Borussia.

Right: Sir Bert Millichip had a wonderful life in football. A West Bromwich Albion supporter and then shareholder, he became a director at The Hawthorns in 1964 and ten years later was elected chairman, having been vice-chairman for four years. He resigned in 1983 owing to FA commitments and when he left the board in 1984 he was duly made club president. In 1991 he was knighted (for services to football). Previously a member of the FA Council, he resigned as chairman of the FA in 1996 but continued as president of Albion. A fine cricketer with West Bromwich Dartmouth, he died in 2003 after a long and wonderful innings.

Above left: Birmingham-born midfielder Paul Devlin started his Football League career with Notts County in 1992. After scoring 31 goals for the Magpies (in 180 games) he moved to St Andrew's in February 1996, signed by Barry Fry. Always a 'Blue-nose' he netted 34 times in 89 appearances before joining Sheffield United in 1998, later going back to Meadow Lane and having a second spell with Blues (from February 2002), adding 4 more goals to his tally (in 48 outings). He also gained 5 caps for Scotland prior to his departure.

Above right: During his first spell with West Bromwich Albion (1997-2001) former Kidderminster Harriers striker Lee Hughes scored 85 goals in 177 senior games. He then had a season with Coventry City before returning to The Hawthorns and duly helping the Baggies regain their Premiership status. Early in 2004 he netted the 100th League goal of his career and when the season ended he was on the brink of the century mark for Albion. This was, however, cut short when he was convicted and imprisoned for a serious driving offence in 2004.

The next three pages consist of pictures of some of the best-known managers in West Midlands football. *Clockwise from top left:*

Ron Atkinson – West Bromwich Albion (1978-81 and 1987-88), Aston Villa (1991-94).

John Barnwell – Wolves (1978-81), Walsall (1989-90).

Alan Buckley – Walsall (1979-86), West Bromwich Albion (1994-97).

Trevor Francis – Birmingham City (1996-2001).

Clockwise from top left:

Barry Fry – Birmingham City (1993-96).

John Gregory – Aston Villa (1998-2002).

Kenny Hibbitt – Walsall (1990-94).

Colin Lee – Wolves (1998-2000), Walsall (2002-04).

Clockwise from top left:

Brian Little – Wolves (1986), Aston Villa (1994-98), West Bromwich Albion (2000).

Ron Saunders – Aston Villa (1974-82), Birmingham City (1982-86), West Bromwich Albion (1986-87).

Graham Taylor – Aston Villa (1987-90 and 2002-03), Wolves (1994-95).

Graham Turner – Aston Villa (1984-86), Wolves (1986-94).

Four players who have all been associated with Aston Villa and are still in the game today. *Clockwise from top left:*

Striker Martin Carruthers left Villa Park for Stoke City in 1993 and has since served with Peterborough United, York City, Darlington, Southend United and Scunthorpe United. He scored the 100th senior goal of his career in 2003.

England international Paul Merson made his debut for Arsenal in 1985 and after spells with Brentford (loan) and Middlesbrough he moved to Villa Park in 1998 for £6.75m. Scorer of 19 goals in 144 outings for Villa he switched to Walsall in 2002, becoming caretaker-manager at the Bescot Stadium in April 2004, and player-manager soon afterwards.

David James played for Watford and Liverpool (277 appearances) before joining Villa for £1.8m in 1999. After 85 starts he was transferred to West Ham United for £3.5m in 2001 and moved to Manchester City in the summer of 2003. He lost his England place in 2004.

Striker Julian Joachim netted 31 goals for Leicester City prior to his £2.2m transfer to Aston Villa in 1996. An England Under-21 international, he added a further 45 goals to his tally (in 173 games) at Villa Park before transferring to Coventry City in July 2001.

Players who were associated with West Bromwich Albion and are still in the game today. *Clockwise from top left:*

Rugged centre half Tony Butler served with Gillingham, Blackpool and Port Vale before joining his former manager Gary Megson at The Hawthorns in March 2000. He made 81 appearances at the heart of the Baggies' defence up to his transfer (after a loan spell) to Bristol City in 2002.

Attacking midfielder/defender Paul Groves was an Alan Buckley signing for Albion in 1996. He netted 5 goals in 32 outings for the Baggies before returning to Grimsby Town. Having started his career with Leicester City, he has also played for Lincoln City and Blackpool and Scunthorpe United (his current club).

Utility forward James Quinn made 4 appearances for Blues before moving to Blackpool in 1993. A Northern Ireland international, he scored 48 goals for the Seasiders and had a spell with Stockport prior to joining Albion for £500,000 in 1998. Also with Notts County and Bristol Rovers, he is currently with the Dutch club, Willem II.

Injuries apart, striker Jason Roberts scored 27 goals in 101 games for Albion (2000-03). Signed by Wolves from Barnet, he made no headway at Molineux and after loan spells with Torquay and Bristol City, hit 48 goals for Bristol Rovers before joining the Baggies for £2m, later assisting Portsmouth and Wigan Athletic (signed in 2004).

Birmingham City were the first Midland club to reach the final of a major European competition. In March 1960 they faced the Spanish giants Barcelona in the final of the Inter Cities Fairs Cup and in September 1961 took on the Italian outfit AS Roma in the final of the same tournament. The 'first' ICFC competition was spread over two seasons, commencing in October 1958 and finishing in May 1960. It was run on a knock-out basis (all two-legged rounds) and Blues knocked out, in turn, the West German side FC Cologne (2-2 and 2-0 for a 4-2 aggregate win), Dinamo Zagreb from Czechoslovakia (1-0 and 3-3 for a 4-3 aggregate victory) and Union St Gilloise from Luxembourg (4-2 and 4-2 for a comprehensive 8-4 aggregate scoreline). They then faced Barcelona in the final and saw the Spaniards triumph, winning 4-1 in front of 75,000 fans in the Nou Camp, after a 0-0 draw in front of 40,524 fans at St Andrew's.

The 1960/61 competition took place over a period of twelve months (October to October). Starting off with a 5-3 aggregate win over the Hungarian side Ujpesti Dozsa (3-2 and 2-1), Blues then accounted for the Norwegian club Boldklub Copenhagen (4-4 and 5-0, going through 9-4 on aggregate) before meeting Inter Milan in the semi-final. Crowds of 20,000 in Italy and 29,530 at St Andrew's saw Blues win both legs with 2-1 scorelines to go on and meet another Italian club, AS Roma, in the final. Only 21,005 attended the first leg in Birmingham. It ended 2-2 and Blues knew they had it all to do in Rome. They battled hard and long in front of a 50,000 crowd but went down 2-0 – thus losing their second successive ICFC final in the space of seventeen months.

Above: In the 1950s most football clubs upgraded their official matchday programmes, adding extra pages with colour fronts. Gradually they got better and better and, during the 1960s, a serious collectors' club was introduced as supporters considered that a programme was a valuable part of the club's history. Here are programmes from each of the five major West Midlands clubs from the 1960s.

Opposite: Very few major international or indeed representative matches have been staged in the West Midlands, Villa Park being the main venue, having staged almost 20 full internationals (commencing in 1899), including 1966 World Cup and 1996 European Championship games plus the 1999 European Cup-Winners' Cup final. Two England internationals have taken place at St Andrew's (1922 and 1941) while The Hawthorns has staged three (1922, 1924 and 1945) and Molineux four (1891, 1902, 1936 and 1956). Villa Park, The Bescot Stadium, St Andrew's, Molineux and The Hawthorns have all housed intermediate internationals (i.e. 'B', Under-21 and Under-23) with Villa Park also staging more than 50 FA Cup semi-finals and a League Cup final. Albion have also played hosts to Iraq and Trinidad & Tobago (2004).

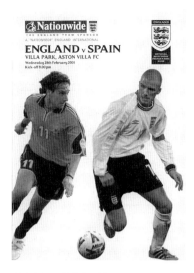 

Clockwise from top left:

In 2001 England beat Spain 3-0 at Villa Park in front of 42,129 spectators.

In this 'B' international at St Andrew's in 1957, a crowd of 39,658 saw England defeat Scotland 4-1.

There were 20,530 fans present to see England beat Greece 5-0 in an Under-23 international at St Andrew's in 1962.

When England 'B' beat Australia 'B' 1-0 at St Andrew's in 1980, only 3,292 hardy supporters turned up – despite there being several Midland-based players in the home line-up.

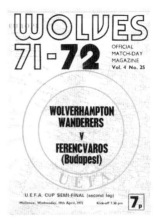

Clockwise from top left:

During the 1950s some of the best teams in Europe visited the Midlands to take on Wolves under the floodlights at Molineux. These included Real Madrid, Moscow Spartak, Moscow Dynamo and Honved. Stan Cullis' Wolves beat all these challengers, a crowd of 55,480 witnessing their 2-1 defeat of Moscow Dynamo in November 1955.

In the 1971/72 season, Wolves became the first Midlands club to reach the final of a major European competition for eleven years. They made progress in the UEFA Cup by knocking out Academica Coimbra (Portugal), FC Den Haag (Holland), Carl Zeiss Jena (East Germany), Juventus (Italy) and Ferencvaros (Hungary) before losing to Spurs in the two-legged final.

West Bromwich Albion toured The People's Republic of China in the summer of 1978. The following year the Chinese national team visited The Hawthorns for a 'return' fixture and as they had done previously, Ron Atkinson's Baggies beat their guests from the Orient quite comfortably 4-0 in front of 11,382 spectators.

In 1977/78 Aston Villa played in the UEFA Cup and reached the quarter-finals where they met Barcelona over two legs. A crowd of 49,619 saw the teams fight out a 2-2 draw at Villa Park and then 90,000 fans packed the Nou Camp for the return leg when the Spaniards won 2-1 to go through 4-3 on aggregate.

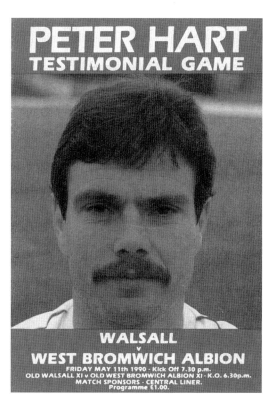

Above left: Walsall moved from their Fellows Park home to the Bescot Stadium in the summer of 1990. The Saddlers' last first-team game at the 'Park' was a testimonial against West Bromwich Albion for long-serving defender and skipper Peter Hart, played on 11 May 1990, when a disappointing crowd of 2,190 witnessed the 1-1 draw.

Above right: The opening fixture at the Bescot Stadium took place three months later, on 18 August, when Aston Villa were the visitors. Virtually a capacity crowd of 9,551 attended to see Villa win 4-0.

Right: The last-ever Football League game at The Victoria Ground, Stoke took place on Sunday 4 May 1997 when West Bromwich Albion were the visitors. A crowd of 22,495 saw the Potters win 2-1. Albion had been the first team to play a League game on that same ground when they beat Stoke 2-0 on 8 September 1888 – 109 years earlier.

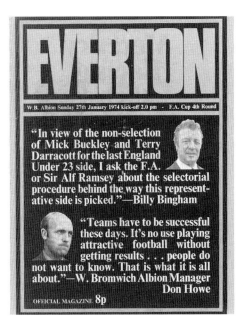

The first competitive Sunday fixtures in this country took place in 1973/74, but the law at the time meant that supporters had to purchase a team-sheet to enter any ground as no payment was taken at the gate. On 27 January 1974 Second Division West Bromwich Albion visited First Division Everton in the fourth round of the FA Cup. A then record 'Sunday' crowd of over 53,000 saw the Baggies put up a terrific fight to force a 0-0 draw and then went on to win the Hawthorns replay 1-0 with a Tony Brown goal. Here is the programme and team-sheet insert for the encounter on Merseyside.

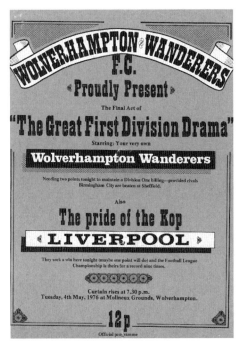

On Tuesday 4 May 1976, relegation-threatened Wolverhampton Wanderers met Championship-seeking Liverpool at Molineux in what was described as 'The Great First Division Drama'. To retain their First Division status, Wolves had to win and Birmingham City lose (at Sheffield United)... if that happened then QPR and not Liverpool would take the title. If Wolves lost or drew (except 3-3 or higher) then Liverpool would be crowned Champions. A tense, packed crowd of 48,918 saw Steve Kindon fire Wolves into a fourteenth-minute lead as news came through that Blues had gone a goal down at Bramall Lane. Liverpool, the most composed and efficient side in the land, gradually pushed Wolves back, but the home side held on – that is until the 77th minute when Kevin Keegan equalised. Wolves drove men forward, left holes at the back allowing John Toshack and Ray Kennedy to nip in and score twice more to earn the Reds a 3-1 win and the title while sending the Wanderers crashing through the trapdoor and into the Second Division.

  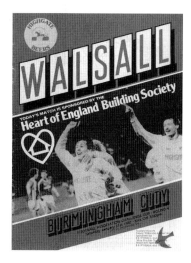

Above left: In 1976 West Bromwich Albion (beaten finalists in 1955 and 1969) won the FA Youth Cup for the first time by beating Wolves comfortably over two legs. Having won 2-0 at Molineux the Baggies eased home 3-0 in the return game at The Hawthorns for an aggregate 5-0 victory.

Above centre: In April 1981, with the League Championship in their sights, Aston Villa met rivals West Bromwich Albion in a vital six-pointer at Villa Park. At the time Villa (53 points) were just ahead of Ipswich Town (52 points) at the top of the table with Albion still in with an outside chance of taking the title (third on 47). A crowd of almost 48,000 packed into the ground and many were leaving with time running out when Brendon Batson's back pass fell short of his 'keeper allowing Peter Withe to race on and score the winning goal (1-0). Villa never looked back after that gift!

Above right: In January 1987, Third Division Walsall met Second Division Birmingham City in a fourth round FA Cup-tie at Fellows Park and in front of almost 15,000 spectators the Saddlers caused a minor upset by winning 1-0 thanks to a Nicky Cross goal.

Right: In September 1992 fourth-placed Birmingham City met Wolves (third) in a First Division game at St Andrew's. A crowd of 14,391 attended for what was likely to be a tight contest. This was not to be the case, however...Wolves won comfortably by 4-0 with Darren Roberts, playing in only his second League game, scoring a hat-trick while Steve Bull netted the other.

Other football titles published by Tempus

Aston Villa Football Club
TONY MATTHEWS

From their founding by members of the Wesleyan Chapel cricket team in the 1870s, Aston Villa have gone from strength to strength. This book illustrates the Villans' history and includes many great achievements, such as the winning of the double in 1897 (which was followed by many more domestic triumphs) and the lifting of the European Cup in the 1980s, as well as the current stars of the Premiership.
0 7524 3123 4

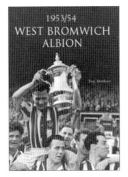

West Bromwich Albion A Season to Remember 1953/54
TONY MATTHEWS

Fifty years ago, West Bromwich Albion had what could be described as their greatest season ever as they came within a whisker of the coveted double by winning the FA Cup and finishing runners-up in the First Division to neighbours and rivals Wolverhampton Wanderers. The side of 1953/54, under the shrewd management of Vic Buckingham, produced a brilliant style of football – attractive, full of movement, concise and a joy to watch.
0 7524 3124 2

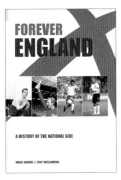

Forever England
MARK SHAOUL & TONY WILLIAMSON

The definitive history of the English national side. From the days of the amateur gentlemen of the 1870s to the present day, *Forever England* is an insightful and fascinating illustrated account of the history of the national football team which covers the careers of England's all-time greats and is an essential read for anyone who is interested in the history of the Three Lions.
0 7524 2939 6

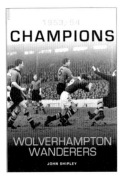

Wolverhampton Wanderers Champions 1953/54
JOHN SHIPLEY

On 24 April 2004, Wolves celebrated the fiftieth anniversary of their first ever League Championship: the first of a hat-trick of Championships they were to win in the fabulous '50s. This is the story of that incredible season, recounted game by game, as Wolves successfully fought off a concerted challenge from one of their biggest rivals – that other club from the Black Country, West Bromwich Albion.
0 7524 3234 6

If you are interested in purchasing other books published by Tempus, or in case you have difficulty finding any Tempus books in your local bookshop, you can also place orders directly through our website

www.tempus-publishing.com